Introduction

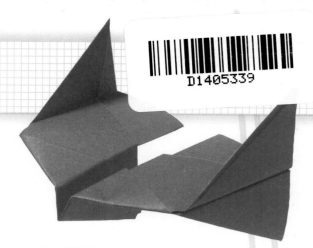

Paper planes

Paper aeroplanes are a one-way ticket back to your childhood! Paper planes are the perfect hobby or interest for people of all ages, backgrounds and level of expertise. Plane making is both stimulating and relaxing. It costs virtually nothing, needs no equipment and is a low-tech way to have a lot of fun. You can choose to make designs as easy or as relatively difficult as you wish; either way gives a real sense of achievement. Create your planes on your own, as a family or as a small group and see how fast, high and long they can fly. Above all, have fun with them!

In *Paper Planes That Really Fly!* there are plenty of designs for you to try. I give step-by-step instructions for 40 planes, many of which are original designs that you won't find anywhere else! Once you have mastered the steps, you are only a piece of paper away from launching your newest creation.

The designs become more complicated as you go through the book, often building on earlier ideas, so if you start at the beginning you should find it easier to tackle the more complex constructions. Alternatively, you can dive right in and start making the planes that most appeal to you. Perhaps you will even be inspired to create some designs of your own!

A brief history of paper aeroplanes

The first real aeroplane was designed, built and flown in 1903 by the Wright brothers. As far as I can tell, the earliest documented paper aeroplane followed ten years later, in 1913. I am still searching for earlier paper aeroplane designs; I have read about some from as early as 700 AD!

Some of the first pilots, the 'Early Birds', created some very nice paper aeroplane designs. A standout is Percy Pierce. His patented designs appeared in issues of American women's fashion magazines *McCall's* and *The Delineator* in the 1920s. The planes were quite striking, and fairly complex to assemble.

During the 1940s, great advances occurred in aviation. Planes flew faster and higher, and were more reliable than ever. In this decade the jet engine was born, and all metal planes reigned supreme. As a consequence, the increased knowledge of avionics also improved paper planes. Paper planes became so popular that designs were even featured on cereal boxes. A key designer of the day was Wallis Rigby, who is credited with creating the 'tab and slot' method. His planes appeared in newspapers, thrilling readers with their realistic detail. Even today they are a lot of fun to make and fly.

The Great International Paper Airplane Book, published in 1967, introduced the concept of laminate paper aeroplanes, which were popularised by Dr Yasuaki Ninomiya of Japan in his famous and fantastic *Whitewings* series. Capable of greater speeds, heights and variety of shapes, some of the models were even propelled by a rubber band launcher, which could catapult them high enough to ride thermals!

A further significant development occurred in the 1970s when Americans Richard Kline and Floyd Fogleman came up with a new airfoil design using paper aeroplanes as a test bed. Their unique wing shape could also change its thickness, and they eventually patented the concept, which was quite a feat! Their 1985 book, *The Ultimate Paper Airplane*, provides plans for seven different models of this groundbreaking design.

Paper aeroplane competitions

The first international paper aeroplane competition was held in 1967, sponsored and conducted by *Scientific American*. The competition brought together various styles and forms of paper aeroplane making from all over the world, which were subsequently published in *The Great*

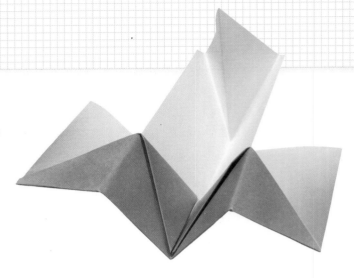

International Paper Airplane Book. The book became a bestseller and many of its designs are among those that are most recognised today.

In 1985 the second international paper aeroplane contest was held. Conducted by the editors of *Science 86* magazine, it demonstrated how many advances had been made since the first contest eighteen years previously.

The World Record

Takuo Toda, Chairman of the Japan Origami Airplane Association, is the current title holder of the Guinness World Record for time aloft of a paper aeroplane. He set the record in April 2009, with a time of 27.9 seconds. Prior to Mr Toda breaking the World Record, Ken Blackburn, an aeronautical engineer living in Laurel Hill, Florida, flew a paper plane inside the USA's Georgia Dome in 1998 and held the record of 27.6 seconds for over 10 years!

A note on paper

The designs in this book were created with and for 75gsm (20lb) sheets of A4 paper. While this size is very popular, it is by no means the only kind of paper you can use. A size close to A4 is Letter, which is a little shorter and wider than A4. You can still create the designs in this book with Letter size, just keep in mind that the angles on some of the illustrations may not match up, and that the finished plane may need additional tweaking and trimming to fly correctly.

You can have plenty of fun experimenting with different types of paper – variations in size, thickness and rigidity will all produce different results. For example, some planes are constructed from square sheets of A4 paper. To make your own square sheets, fold the top left corner of the paper over to the right side, keeping the top edge of the paper even with the right side. Give it a good crease so the paper will stay in place, then cut off the excess paper on the bottom. Unfold, and you've got your square.

Don't forget to make your plane look good too! Use coloured paper, stickers, patterned paper, or draw your favourite designs onto your plane to make it stand out.

About the author

Growing up in Iowa, Dean Mackey always enjoyed flying paper aeroplanes. Some of his earliest memories are of flying paper aeroplanes off the porch and watching them soar over the cliff across the street. His older siblings taught him a few designs, and he learnt a few more from the venerable *Great International Paper Airplane Book*.

Dean's skills lay dormant until the year 2000, when he volunteered to work at 'Space Day' in Tewksbury, Massachusetts. Researching new designs, Dean was amazed at what he found on the internet. As well as experimenting with his own designs, he started collecting web links that talented people had put online for all to enjoy. A few years later, he launched The Online Paper Airplane Museum, featuring over 800 free paper aeroplane designs, personal reviews of paper aeroplane books, and many other items related to paper planes.

Visit The Online Paper Airplane Museum at http://www.theonlinepaperairplanemuseum.com. Questions or comments can be sent to Dean at deanmackey@gmail.com.

This book is dedicated to Katie (Schmoopie) Mackey.

Aviation Glossary

AILERON

A movable panel at the rear edge of each aeroplane wing; the aileron can be raised or lowered and cause the plane to bank left or right.

AIRFOIL

The shape of the wing as seen from the side; it is the shape of the wing that causes a plane to lift.

CANARD

A small wing that sits forward of the main wings on the fuselage of a plane.

DIHEDRAL

The position of the wings on a plane relative to the fuselage. If the wings are raised relative to the fuselage, the dihedral is positive. If the wings are lowered, the dihedral is negative.

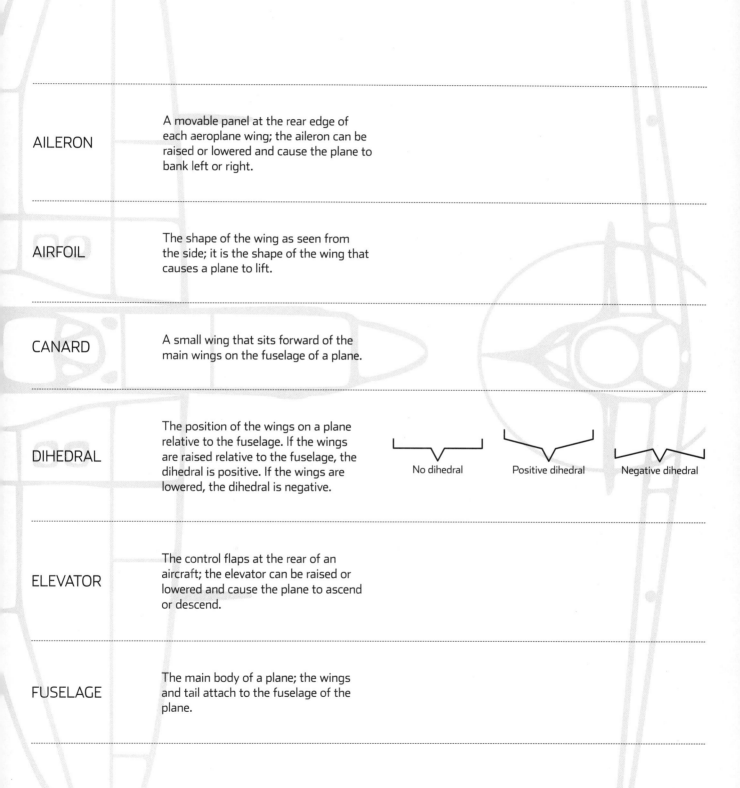

No dihedral   Positive dihedral   Negative dihedral

ELEVATOR

The control flaps at the rear of an aircraft; the elevator can be raised or lowered and cause the plane to ascend or descend.

FUSELAGE

The main body of a plane; the wings and tail attach to the fuselage of the plane.

Aviation Glossary

RUDDER

A vertical airfoil at the tail of a plane used for steering; the rudder can be moved left or right and cause the plane to move right or left.

SPOILER

A small airfoil, usually found on the rear of a racing car. On the planes in this book, a spoiler is intended to increase lift.

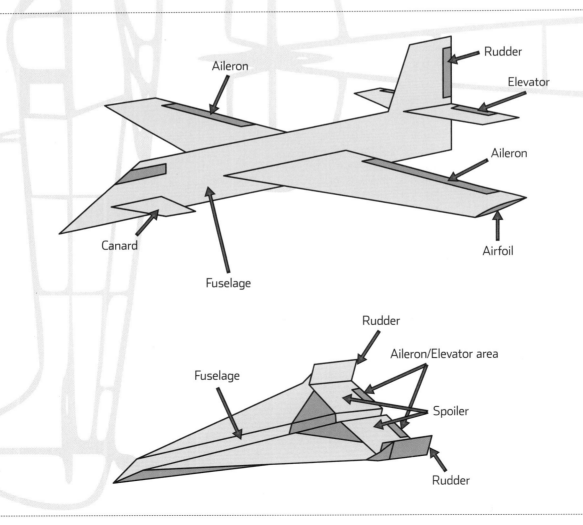

Aileron

Rudder

Elevator

Aileron

Airfoil

Canard

Fuselage

Rudder

Aileron/Elevator area

Fuselage

Spoiler

Rudder

Folding Glossary

FLIP FOLD

Fold up along the result of a previous fold.

INSIDE REVERSE FOLD

The corner of an existing fold is creased, pushed in and folded on the inside.

MOUNTAIN FOLD

Fold sides together so paper forms a ∧ shape.

PRESS

Use your fingers to push the paper in the correct direction.

PRESS FOLD

Bring two creases together and press down the excess paper that is curved between them to create a new crease.

 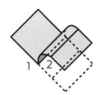

REVERSE FOLD

The corner of an existing fold is creased, reversed and folded over to the outside.

Folding Glossary

SQUASH FOLD

Start with at least two layers of paper. Make creases in the top layer. Lift the top layer, move it across and then press down on the creases.

TAP

Use your finger and tap where indicated to set off a preset series of folds.

TRIM

The final adjustments to a paper plane so that it flies straight and true. This may involve adjustments to the ailerons, elevator and rudder.

VALLEY FOLD

Fold sides together so paper forms a V shape.

Simple Flying Wing

This is one of the most basic of all paper aeroplanes. Composed solely of two wings, it has no tail, fuselage, or rudder. Be careful to make all the folds even, as too much deviation will result in an unstable flyer. Made correctly, the Simple Flying Wing is a good, stable glider. Examples of it can be seen in aviation, most prominently in the Northrop Flying Wing series.

1

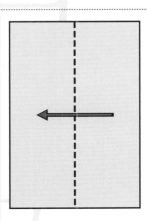

Begin with a sheet of A4 paper.

2

Fold the left side over to and even with the right side.

3

Unfold.

4

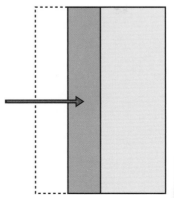

Fold the left side over to the centre crease.

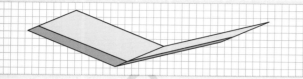

Simple Flying Wing

5

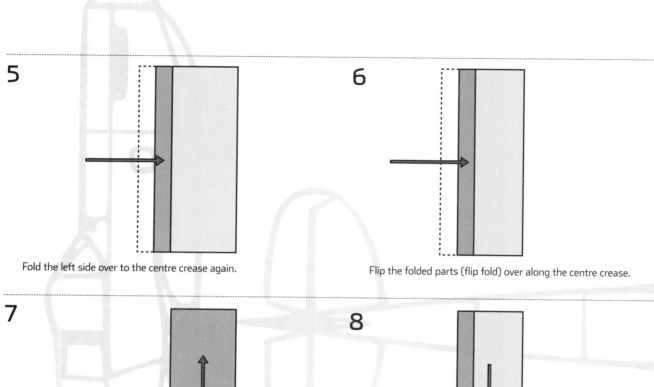

Fold the left side over to the centre crease again.

6

Flip the folded parts (flip fold) over along the centre crease.

7

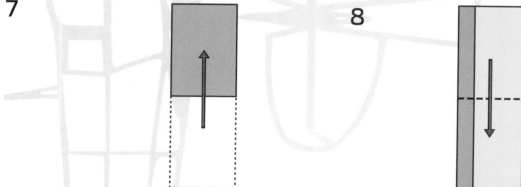

Fold up from the bottom edge to the top edge.

8

Unfold.

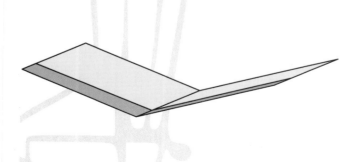

In the air, the Simple Flying Wing should have a slight positive dihedral, as shown. To launch, grasp the plane from the back, lift it as high as you can, and release.

Standard

Here is a plane design that is truly international. I recently met a Russian woman who had made this in her childhood. It is exactly the same design I learned growing up in Iowa. Capable of fast speed and accuracy, the Standard will streak across the sky!

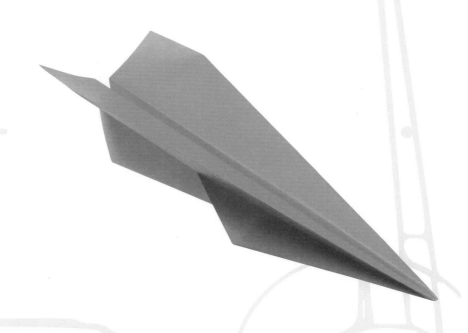

1

Begin with a sheet of A4 paper.

2

Fold the left side over to and even with the right side.

3

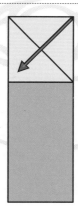

Fold the top right corner down to the left side.

4

Fold the right side over to the left side as shown.

5

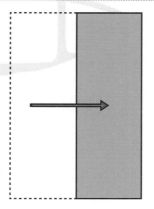

Fold again from the right side over to the left side as shown.

6

Flip over, from left to right.

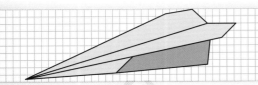

Standard

7

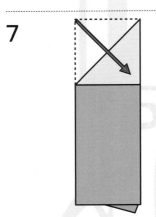

Fold the top left corner down to the right side.

8

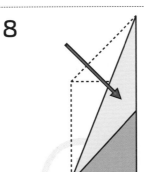

Fold from the left side over to the right side as shown.

9

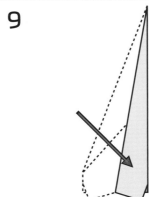

Fold the left side over to the right side again, as shown.

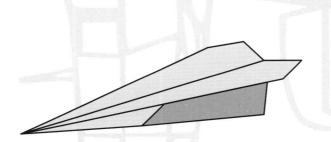

Unfold, and pop up the wings to give a slight positive dihedral, as shown. This plane will fly far and fast if you grasp it along the fuselage and throw it as hard as you can!

Traditional

Another well-known design, the Traditional reverses a lot of the folds of the Standard. It tucks the folds inside to make a more aerodynamic plane, and it also incorporates a couple of wingtip 'rudders' to make it fly straight.

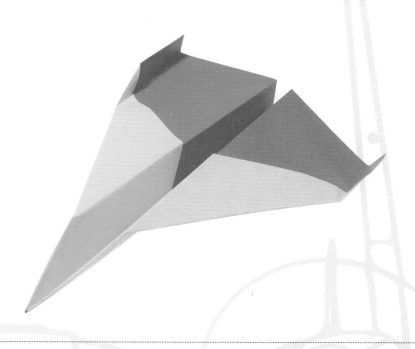

1

Begin with a sheet of A4 paper.

2

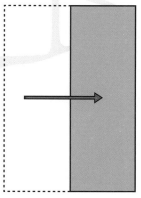

Fold the left side over to and even with the right side.

3

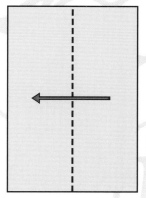

Unfold.

4

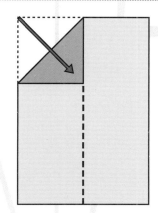

Fold the top left corner down.

5

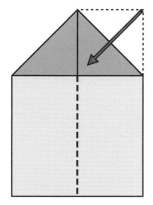

Repeat the same fold with the top right corner.

6

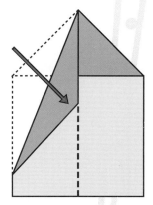

Fold the left side down to the centre.

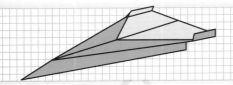

Traditional

7

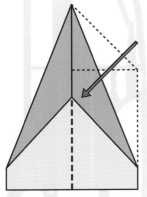

Repeat with the right side.

8

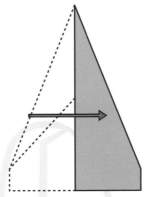

Fold the left side over to and even with the right side.

9

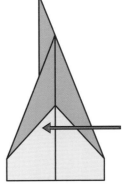

Take the top wing and fold it over to the left, leaving about 3 cm (1.2 inches) of fuselage.

10

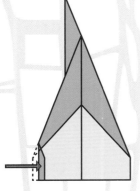

Fold the left wing tip up 1 cm (0.4 inches).

11

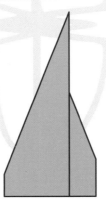

Flip over, from left to right.

12

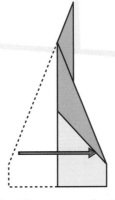

Fold the left wing over to the right, leaving about 3 cm (1.2 inches) of fuselage.

13

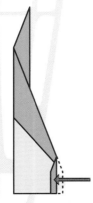

Fold the right wing tip over to the left 1 cm (0.4 inches).

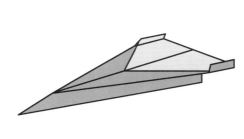

Fold the wings up, and make the wing tips upright. This plane will fly just as hard and fast as you can throw it!

Improved Traditional

This is my improved version of the Traditional. It features a thicker airfoil for a smoother, stable flight. It will need a little up elevator, but with some practice you will be rewarded with a great flying plane!

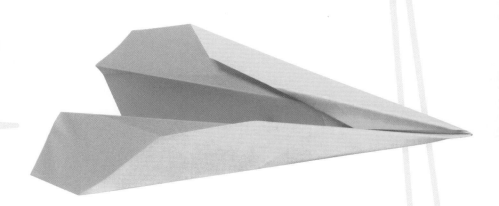

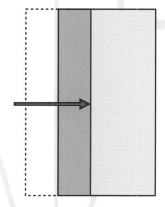

1

Begin with a sheet of A4 paper.

2

Fold the left side over to and even with the right side.

3

Unfold.

4

Fold the left side over to the centre.

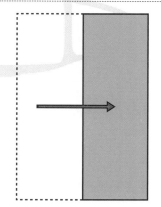

5

Unfold.

6

Fold the right side over to the centre.

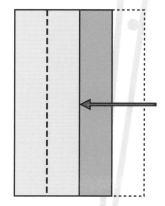

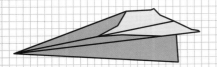

Improved Traditional

7

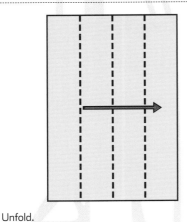

Unfold.

8

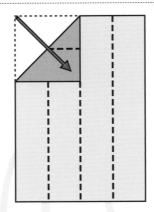

Fold the top left corner down to the centre crease.

9

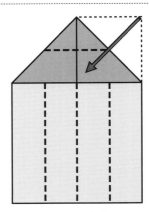

Repeat the same fold with the top right corner.

10

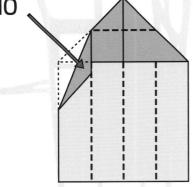

Take the left side and fold to the first crease.

11

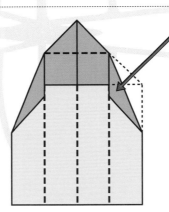

Repeat on the right side, folding to the first crease.

12

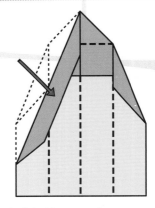

Take the left side over to the centre crease as shown.

13

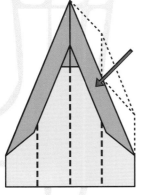

Take the right side over to the centre crease as shown.

14

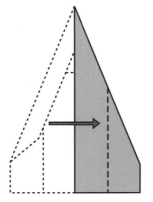

Fold in half from the left side over to and even with the right side.

15

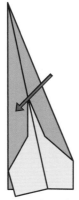

Fold the top wing over from the right side to the left side, keeping it even with the left side.

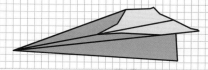

16

Flip over, from left to right.

17

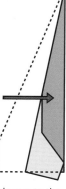

Fold the left side over to the right side, keeping it even with the right side.

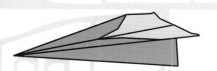

The Improved Traditional has a nice, smooth glide, and can be very accurate! This plane will take as fast a throw as you can muster!

Simple Dart

For a truly speedy flyer, try this little number. With minimal wing area, it has little drag. Of course, that also means that it requires a high airspeed to make it fly.

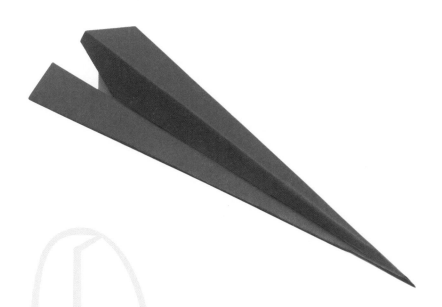

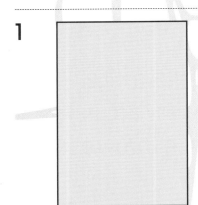

1

Begin with a sheet of A4 paper.

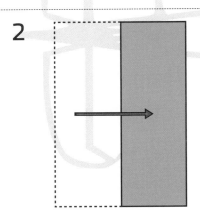

2

Fold the left side over to and even with the right side.

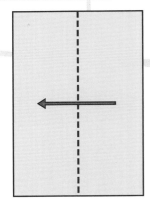

3

Unfold.

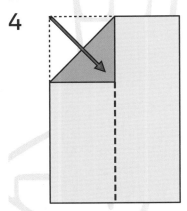

4

Fold the top left corner down.

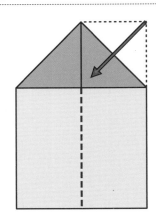

5

Repeat the same fold with the top right corner.

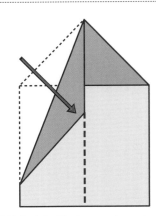

6

Fold the left side down to the centre crease.

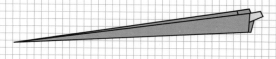

7

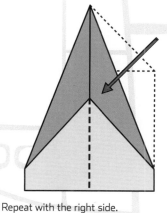

Repeat with the right side.

8

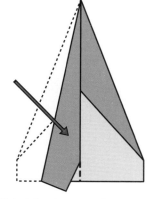

Fold the left side over to the centre crease again.

9

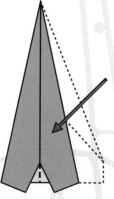

Fold the right side over to the centre crease.

10

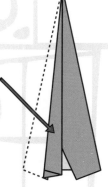

Fold the left side over to the centre.

11

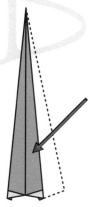

Fold the right side over to the centre.

12

Flip over, from left to right.

13

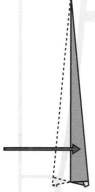

Fold the left side over to the right side.

This is a very sleek and speedy paper aeroplane. Throw with all your strength to make the Simple Dart fly fast and far!

Javelin

Much like the track and field spear this plane is named after, the Javelin is truly meant for distance competitions.

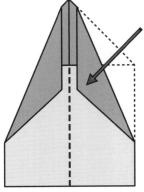

1

Begin with a sheet of A4 paper.

2

Fold the left side over to and even with the right side.

3

Unfold.

4

Fold the top left corner down.

5

Repeat the same fold with the top right corner.

6

Fold the left side in, stopping 1.5 cm (0.6 inches) from the centre crease.

7

Repeat on the right side, stopping 1.5 cm (0.6 inches) from the centre crease.

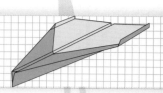

8

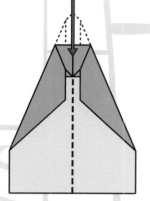

Fold the top down to the line as shown.

9

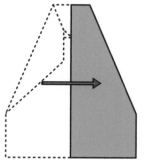

Fold the left side over to and even with the right side.

10

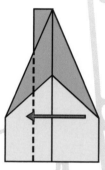

Fold the top wing to the left, starting at the top right corner and keeping the bottom edge even.

11

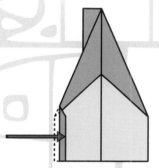

Fold the left side in 1 cm (0.4 inches).

12

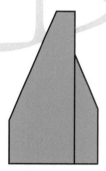

Flip over, from left to right.

13

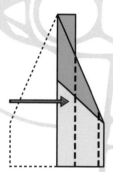

Fold the left side over to the right side, keeping the left edge even with the wing beneath it.

14

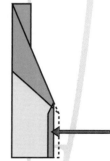

Fold the right side in 1 cm (0.4 inches).

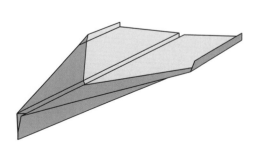

This is a great and graceful distance flyer. It may need a little up elevator, but in still air, the Javelin will fly straight and far!

Middleweight

Not all planes carry all of the weight in the nose. Sometimes you just have to mix things up a bit and try something new!

1

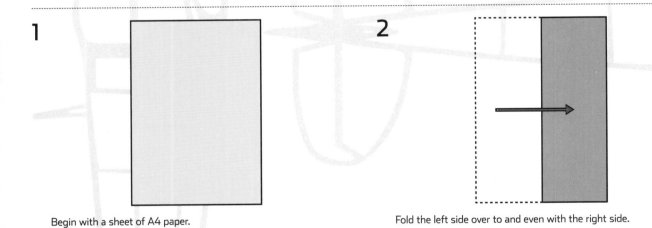

Begin with a sheet of A4 paper.

2

Fold the left side over to and even with the right side.

3

Unfold.

4

Fold the top edge down to and even with the bottom edge.

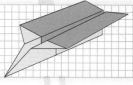

5

Unfold.

6

Flip over, from left to right.

7

Fold the top edge down to the centre.

8

Unfold.

9

Squash fold the centre horizontal crease up to the three-quarter crease.

10

Fold the top left corner down to and even with the vertical centre crease.

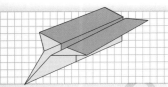

11

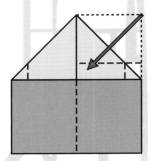

Fold the top right corner down to and even with the vertical centre crease.

12

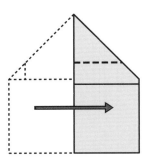

Fold the left side over to and even with the right side.

13

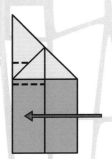

Fold the top right layer over to and even with the left side.

14

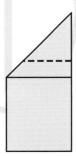

Flip over, from left to right.

15

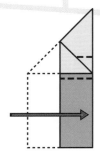

Fold the left side over to and even with the right side.

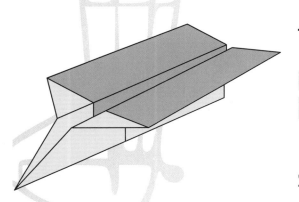

The Middleweight differs from most planes in that a large portion of its balancing weight is near the middle. It will only take a gentle toss to send it soaring across the room!

Doppelganger

At first glance, the Doppelganger looks a lot like the Middleweight. But it is a result of different folds, and it flies a little differently. That is why it is called the Doppelganger, which means 'twin' or 'look-alike'.

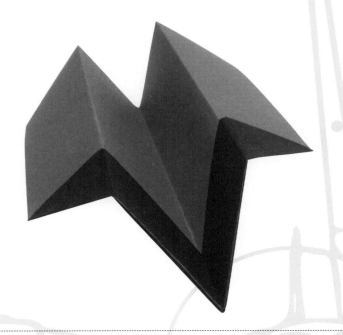

1

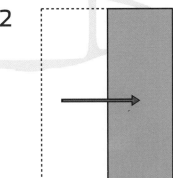

Begin with a sheet of A4 paper.

2

Fold the left side over to and even with the right side.

3

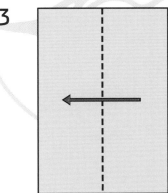

Unfold.

4

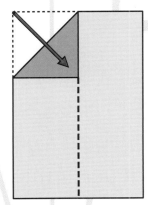

Fold the top left corner down to the centre crease.

5

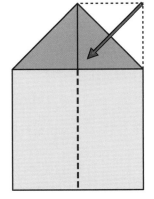

Repeat the fold with the top right corner.

6

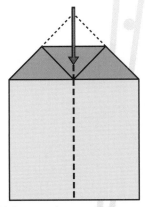

Fold the point down to the line.

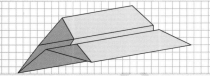

Doppelganger

7
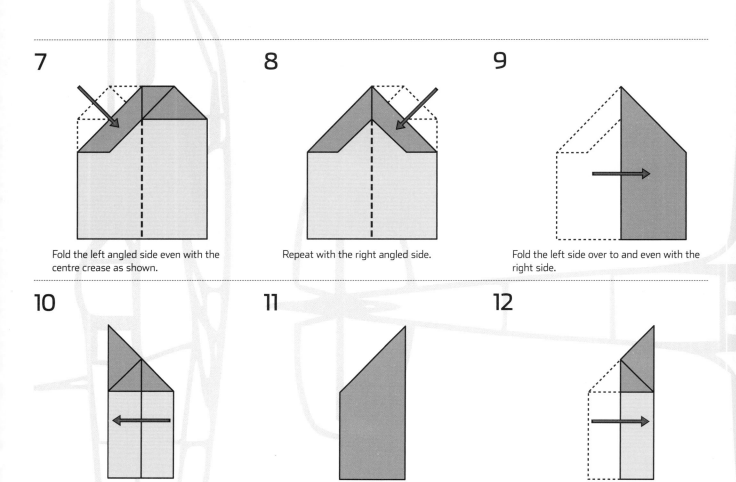
Fold the left angled side even with the centre crease as shown.

8
Repeat with the right angled side.

9
Fold the left side over to and even with the right side.

10
Fold the top wing over to and even with the left side.

11
Flip over, from left to right.

12
Fold the top wing over to and even with the right side.

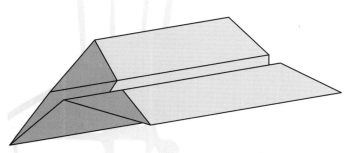

Unlike the Middleweight, the Doppelganger has all of its weight up front. Give it a gentle toss and watch it perform!

Cyrano

Cyrano de Bergerac was a Frenchman who was reputed to have a large nose that he was quite proud of. I think he would be proud of the plane I named after him, which has a large nose too!

1

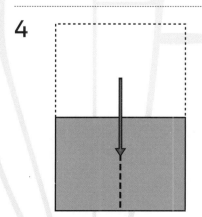

Begin with a sheet of A4 paper.

2

Fold the left side over to and even with the right side.

3

Unfold.

4

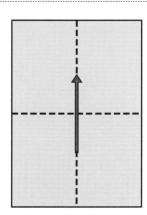

Fold the top edge down to the bottom edge.

5

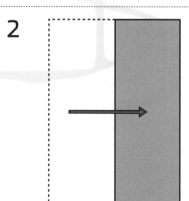

Unfold.

6

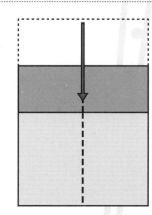

Fold the top down to the centre crease.

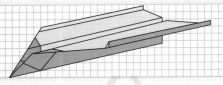

Cyrano

7

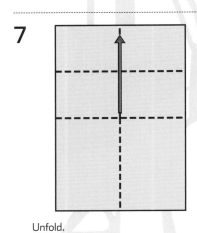

Unfold.

8

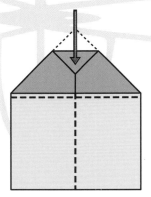

Fold the top down to the crease just created.

9

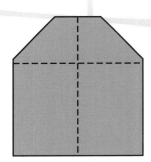

Fold the top left corner down to the centre crease.

10

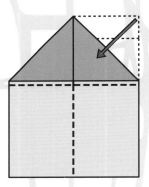

Fold the right corner down to the centre crease.

11

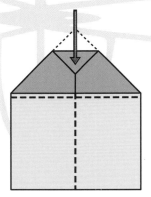

Fold the point down 3.5 cm (1.4 inches).

12

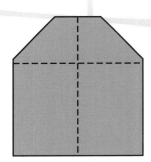

Flip over, from left to right.

13

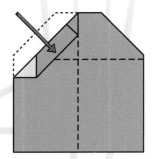

Fold the left angled side to the centre as shown.

14

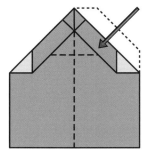

Fold the right angled side over to the centre crease as shown.

15

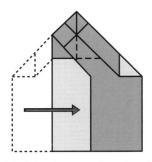

Fold the left side over to the right side 6 cm (2.4 inches).

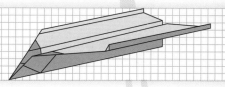

16

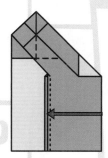

Fold the top wing over to the left 1 cm (0.4 inches).

17

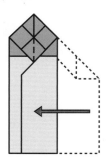

Fold the right side over to the left side 6 cm (2.4 inches).

18

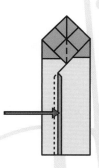

Fold the top wing over to the right 1 cm (0.4 inches).

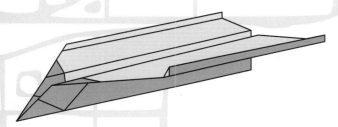

The Cyrano's large nose means it has lots of weight up front so you can throw it harder.

Afterburner

An afterburner is a component of some jet engines, placed after the main engine. Extra fuel is injected into the afterburner and burned for increased thrust. In this paper aeroplane, a spoiler is placed near the end to increase lift. Adding the spoiler to the stabilisers also makes it more stable!

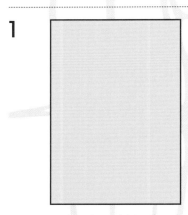

1

Begin with a sheet of A4 paper.

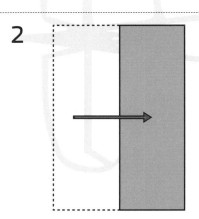

2

Fold the left side over to and even with the right side.

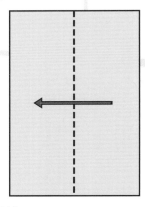

3

Unfold.

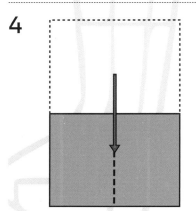

4

Fold the top edge down to the bottom edge.

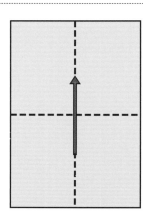

5

Unfold.

6

Fold the bottom edge up to the centre crease.

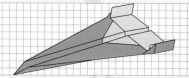

7

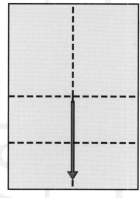

Unfold.

8

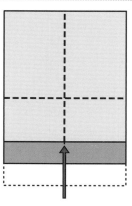

Fold the bottom edge up to the crease just created.

9

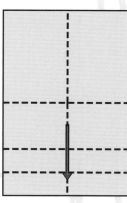

Unfold.

10

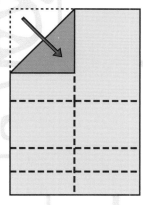

Fold the top left corner down to the vertical centre crease.

11

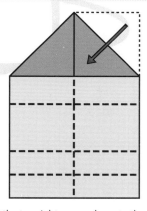

Fold the top right corner down to the vertical centre crease.

12

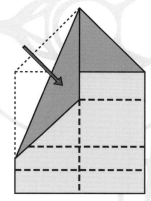

Fold the top left angled side over to the vertical centre crease as shown.

13

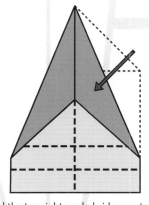

Fold the top right angled side over to the vertical centre crease as shown.

14

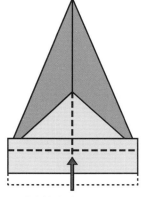

Now squash fold the lowest crease up to the one above it.

15

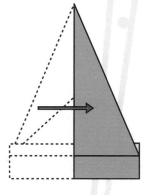

Fold the left side over to and even with the right side.

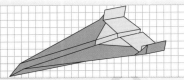

Afterburner

16

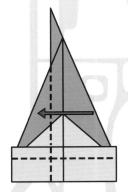

Fold the top wing over to the left, leaving 2 cm (0.8 inches) for the fuselage.

17

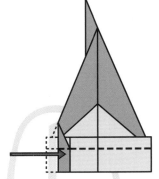

Fold the left side over 2.5 cm (1 inch).

18

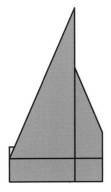

Flip, from left to right.

19

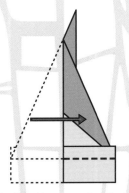

Fold the left side over so that the left side on top matches the fold below.

20

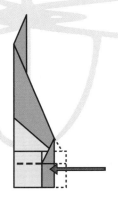

Fold the right side over 2.5 cm (1 inch).

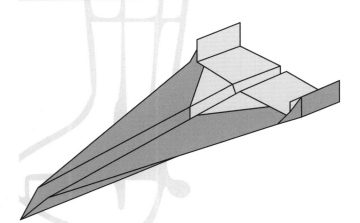

The Afterburner's additional reinforcement in the back provides it with extra lift and accuracy. Use it wisely!

Loopy

A loop is a neat trick for a real pilot in a real plane. It is also a neat trick to perform with a paper aeroplane! The Loopy starts off a lot like others in the first section, but flies differently!

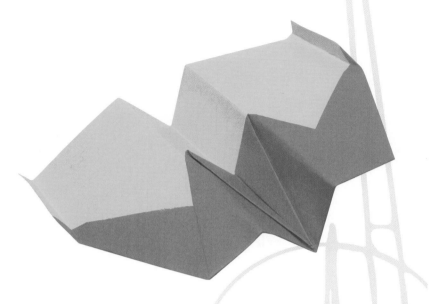

1

Begin with a sheet of A4 paper.

2

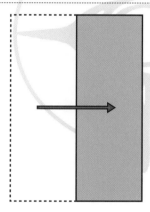

Fold the left side over to and even with the right side.

3

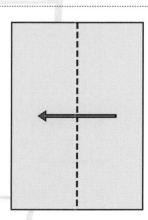

Unfold.

4

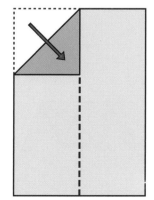

Fold the left corner down to and even with the centre crease.

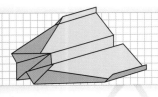

Loopy

5

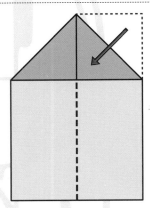

Fold the right corner down to and even with the centre crease.

6

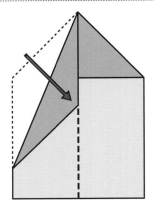

Fold the left angled side down to the centre crease as shown.

7

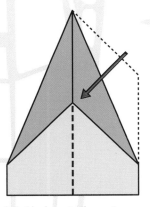

Fold the right angled side down to the centre crease as shown.

8

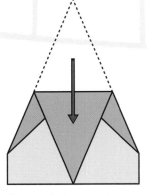

Fold the top point down to the bottom edge.

9

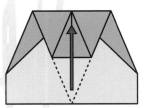

Fold the point back up to the top edge just created.

10

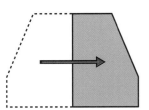

Fold the left side over to and even with the right side.

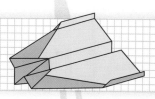

Loopy

11

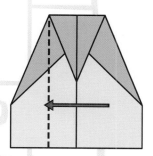

Fold the top right layer over to the left, matching the top right corner over to the top left corner as shown.

12

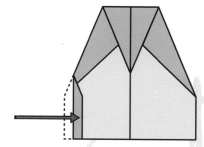

Fold the left side over 1 cm (0.4 inches).

13

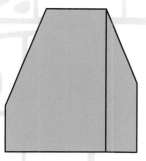

Flip over, from left to right.

14

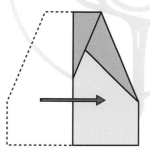

Fold the left side over, matching the centre fold underneath.

15

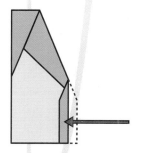

Fold the right side over 1 cm (0.4 inches).

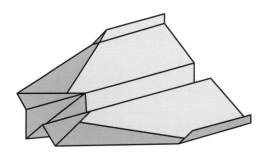

Unfold the wings, perhaps give a little up elevator, and watch Loopy perform!

Acrobatic

Here is another great classic plane. My brothers taught me how to make this one when I was young, and it still is hard to match! Easy to toss in a circle, the Acrobatic is as agile as its name!

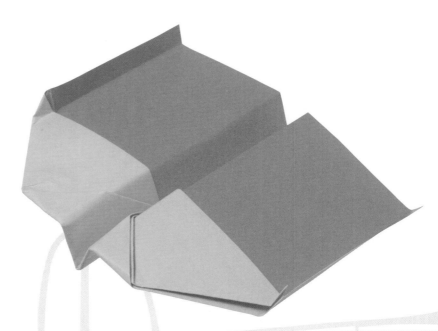

1

Begin with a sheet of A4 paper.

2

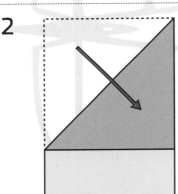

Fold the top left corner down to and even with the right side.

3

Fold the top right corner down the left side.

4

Fold the top down to and even with the layers of paper as shown.

5

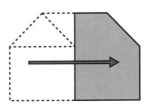

Fold the left side over to and even with the right side.

6

Fold the top right layer over to the left, matching the top right corner to the top left corner as shown.

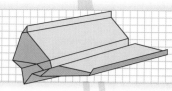

7

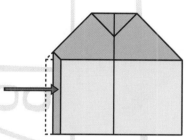

Fold the left side over to the right side
1 cm (0.4 inches).

8

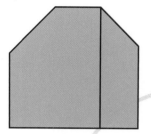

Flip over, from right to left.

9

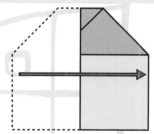

Fold the left side over to the right side,
so that the left edges match up.

10

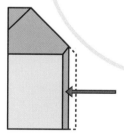

Fold the top wing over to the left
1 cm (0.4 inches).

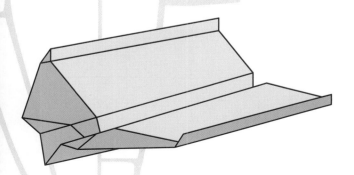

Depending on how you toss it,
the Acrobatic will do a loop,
or it will stall and turn upside
down and then fly back to you!

Small Scout

This little plane reminds me of a spaceship, the kind that spacemen would use to explore new planets. I call it the Small Scout because it is so tiny!

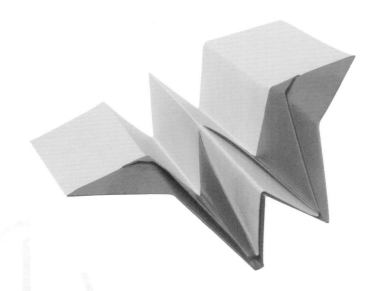

1

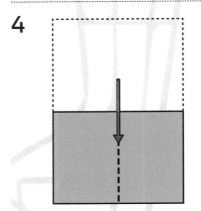

Begin with a sheet of A4 paper.

2

Fold the left side over to and even with the right side.

3

Unfold.

4

Fold the top edge down to and even with the bottom edge.

5

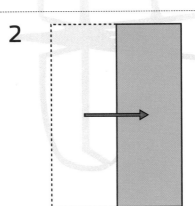

Unfold.

6

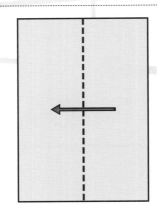

Fold the top edge down to the horizontal centre crease.

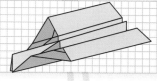

7

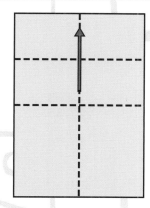

Unfold.

8

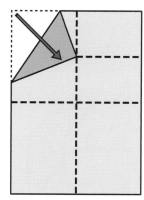

Fold the top left corner down to the top intersection of creases.

9

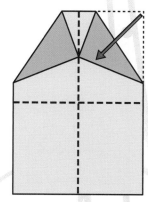

Fold the top right corner down to the top intersection of creases.

10

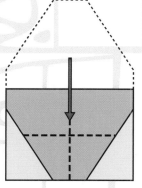

Fold the top edge down to the bottom edge.

11

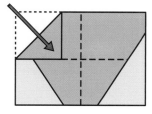

Fold the top left corner down to and even with the crease as shown.

12

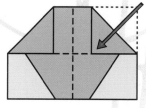

Fold the top right corner down to and even with the crease as shown.

13

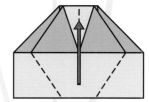

Fold the top layer up from the bottom edge up to the top edge.

14

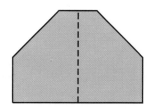

Flip over, from left to right.

15

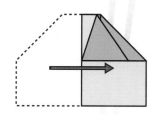

Fold the left side over to and even with the right side.

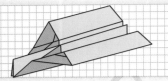

Small Scout

16

Fold the top layer from the right side to the left side, stopping at the top right corner.

17

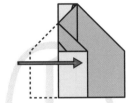

Fold the left side over to the right side, keeping it even with the left side of the layer below as shown.

18

Flip over, from left to right.

19

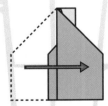

Fold the left side over to the right side, stopping at the top left corner.

20

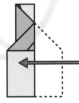

Fold the right side over to the left side, keeping it even with the right side of the layer below.

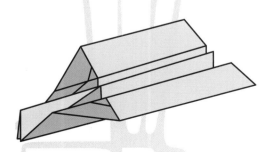

Unfold the stubby little wings out straight, and there you go! Small and speedy, the Small Scout will take a strong throw and keep on going.

Spoiler

Like the Afterburner on page 22, this craft incorporates a spoiler. But the spoiler's so large here, it's practically the whole wing!

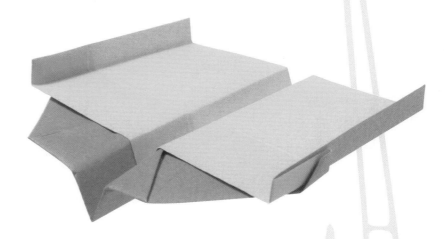

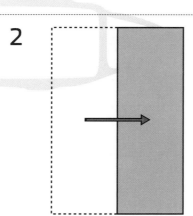

1

Begin with a sheet of A4 paper.

2

Fold the left side over to and even with the right side.

3

Unfold.

4

Fold the top edge down to and even with the bottom edge.

5

Unfold.

6

Fold the top edge down to and even with the centre horizontal crease.

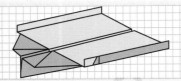

Spoiler

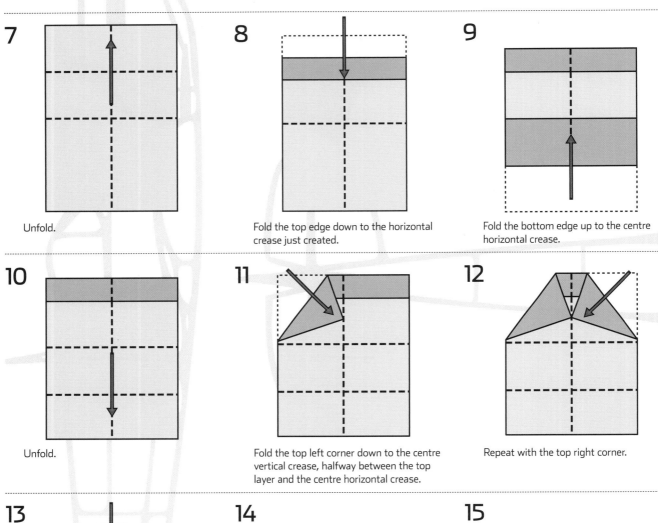

7

Unfold.

8

Fold the top edge down to the horizontal crease just created.

9

Fold the bottom edge up to the centre horizontal crease.

10

Unfold.

11

Fold the top left corner down to the centre vertical crease, halfway between the top layer and the centre horizontal crease.

12

Repeat with the top right corner.

13

Flip fold the top edge along the top layer.

14

Bring the lower horizontal crease up to the centre horizontal crease and then squash fold as shown.

15

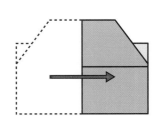

Fold the left side over to and even with the right side.

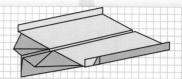

16

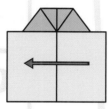

Fold the top layer on the right over to the left by moving the top right corner over to the top left corner as shown.

17

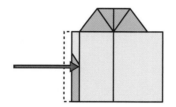

Fold the left side over to where the left angled side starts.

18

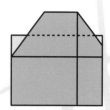

Flip over, from left to right.

19

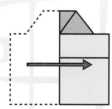

Fold the left side over to the right side, making sure it matches the lower wing on the left side.

20

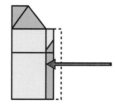

Fold the right side over to the left side, where the right angled side starts.

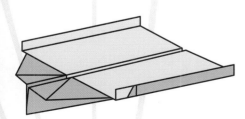

An agile flyer, the Spoiler can really test your limits!

Flying W

Asmooth flyer, this plane doesn't require a hard throw, just a gentle toss to make it glide across the room. It will also come in for a nice landing!

1

Begin with a sheet of A4 paper.

2

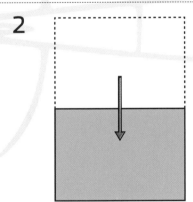

Fold the top edge down to and even with the bottom edge.

3

Unfold.

4

Fold the top left corner down to the centre crease.

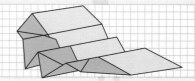

5

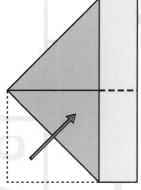

Fold the bottom left corner up to the centre crease.

6

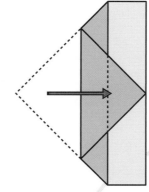

Fold the left point over to the right edge.

7

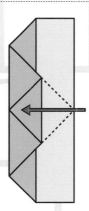

Fold the point back to the left edge just created.

8

Flip over, from top to bottom.

9

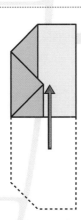

Fold the bottom up to the top edge and crease.

10

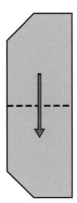

Unfold.

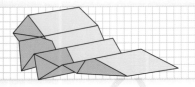

Flying W

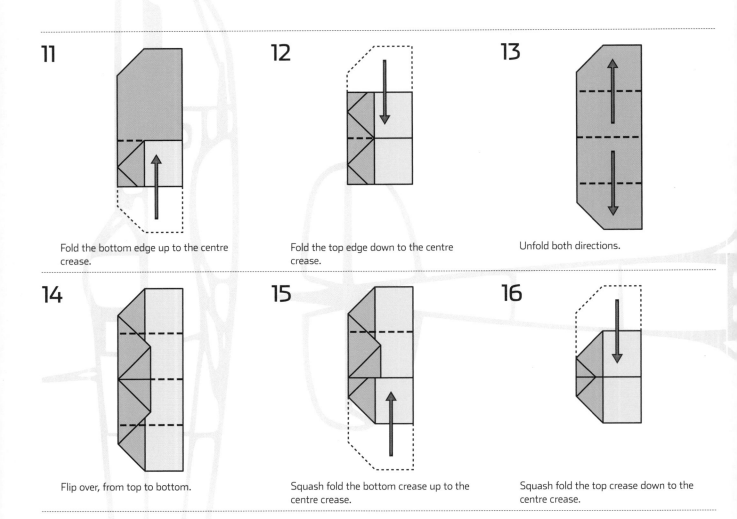

11

Fold the bottom edge up to the centre crease.

12

Fold the top edge down to the centre crease.

13

Unfold both directions.

14

Flip over, from top to bottom.

15

Squash fold the bottom crease up to the centre crease.

16

Squash fold the top crease down to the centre crease.

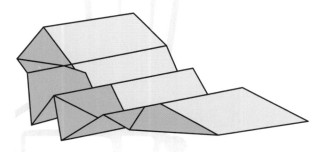

Open up the plane. From the front or the back, it will look like a capital 'W' has sprouted wings!

Slow Jet

A slow jet sounds like an oxymoron, but it's a very apt name for this plane. Slow Jet looks sleek and fast, but it flies so slowly it seems almost stately.

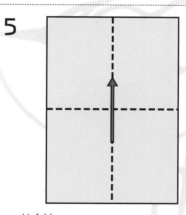

1

Begin with a sheet of A4 paper.

2

Fold the left side over to and even with the right side.

3

Unfold.

4

Fold the top edge down to and even with the bottom edge.

5

Unfold.

6

Fold the bottom edge up to and even with the centre horizontal crease.

7

Unfold.

8

Fold the top left corner down to the centre vertical crease.

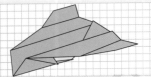

Slow Jet

9

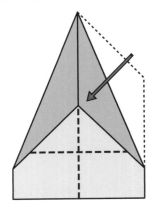

Fold the top right corner down to the centre vertical crease.

10

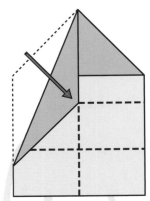

Fold the left angled side over to the centre vertical crease.

11

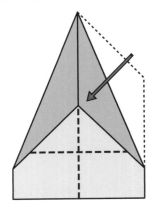

Fold the right angled side over to the centre vertical crease.

12

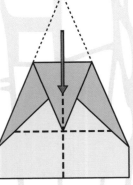

Fold the top point down to the intersection of the creases.

13

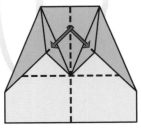

Unfold from below the point outwards as shown.

14

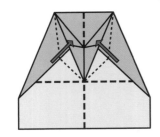

Fold the sides back onto the point as shown.

15

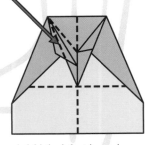

Squash fold the left side as shown.

16

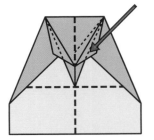

Squash fold the right side as shown.

17

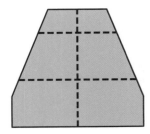

Flip over, from left to right.

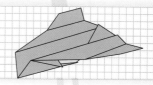

18

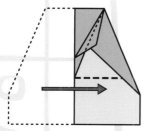

Fold the left side over to the right side.

19

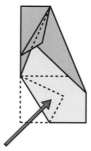

Push fold inside the bottom left corner, creating a tail fin.

20

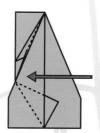

Fold the top layer from the right side over to the left side, using the upper right corner as a pivot.

21

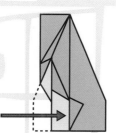

Fold the left side over to the right side, using the last fold as the end point.

22

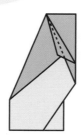

Flip over, from left to right.

23

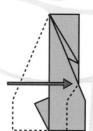

Fold the left side over to the right side, using the upper left corner as a pivot.

24

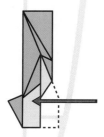

Fold the right side over to the left side, using the last fold as the end point.

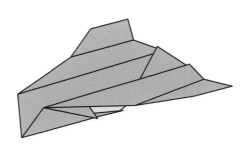

Pop open the wings and square out the lower squash folds. This plane will glide slow and true.

Mantis

With its winglets, this plane reminds me of a praying mantis. It's a tricky flyer, but be patient and you will be rewarded!

1

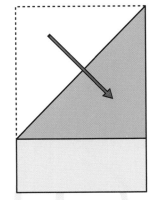

Begin with a sheet of A4 paper.

2

Fold the top left corner down to and even with the right side.

3

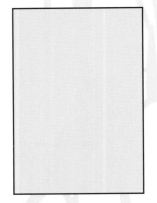

Unfold.

4

Fold the top right corner down to and even with the left side.

5

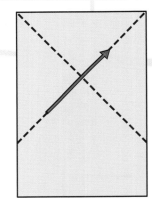

Unfold.

6

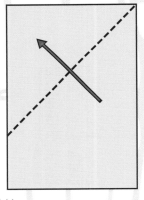

Flip over, from left to right.

7

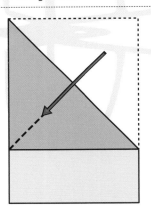

Fold the top down so that it is even with the creases.

8

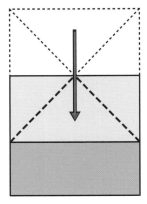

Unfold.

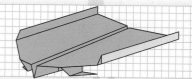

9

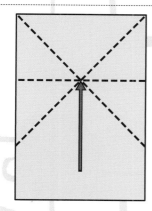

Flip over and press at the centre of all the creases.

10

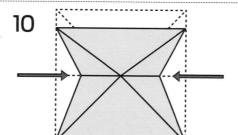

Press the sides in.

11

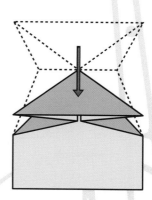

Push down on top, folding in the sides as shown.

12

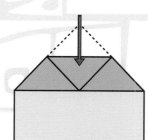

Fold the top point down to the lines formed by the layers of paper.

13

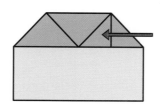

Fold the top flap on the right over to the left.

14

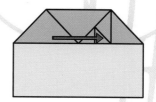

Fold the same flap to the right.

15

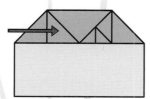

Fold the left flap over to the right.

16

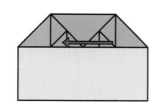

Fold the same flap back to the left.

17

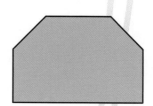

Flip over, from left to right.

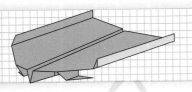

Mantis

18

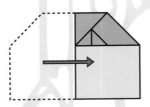

Fold the left side over to and even with the right side.

19

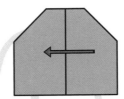

Fold the top layer over to the left side, leaving about 2 cm (0.75 inches) for the fuselage.

20

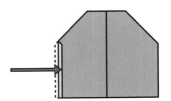

Fold the left side over to the right 1 cm (0.4 inches).

21

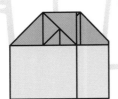

Flip over, from left to right.

22

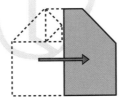

Fold the left side over to the right side, making it even in the centre with the other wing.

23

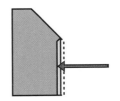

Fold the right side over to the left 1 cm (0.4 inches).

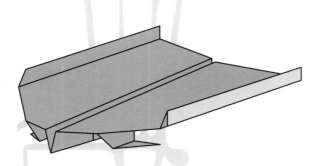

Unfold the winglets below, and keep them even. The Mantis is a temperamental flyer, but can be very acrobatic as well. As a bonus, the winglets act as landing gear!

Little Bug

H ere is the Little Bug! A nice little flyer, it will flit about the room. Little Bug even comes with a pair of legs to stand on when it isn't in the air!

1

Begin with a sheet of A4 paper.

2

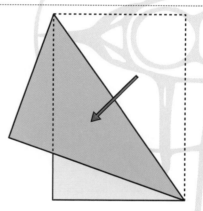

Fold the right side over and crease diagonally from the top left corner to the bottom right corner.

3

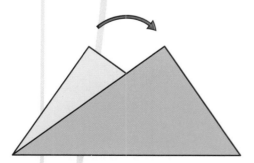

Rotate the paper until the crease is horizontal.

4

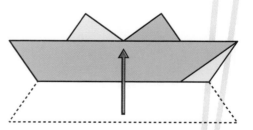

Fold the bottom edge up to the spot between the two points.

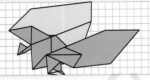

Little Bug

5

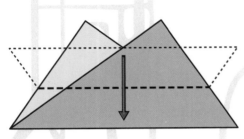

Unfold.

6

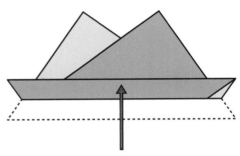

Fold the bottom edge up to the crease just created.

7

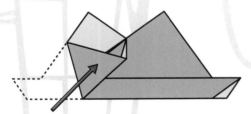

Fold the far left point up to the spot between the two top points as shown.

8

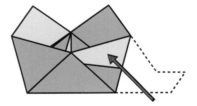

Fold the far right point up to the spot between the two top points as shown.

9

Fold the two triangles in half as shown.

10

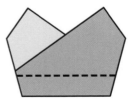

Flip over, from left to right.

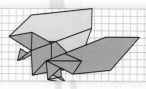

11

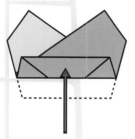

Flip fold up along the crease.

12

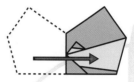

Fold the left side over to and even with the right side.

13

Fold the top right layer over to the left, leaving 3 cm (1.2 inches) behind for the fuselage as shown.

14

Flip over, from left to right.

15

Fold the left side over to and even with the right side.

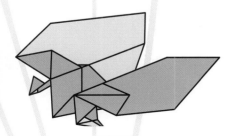

Now pop out the wings and extend the legs below so the Little Bug can stand on its own two feet!

Thick-Winged Delta

A delta wing is a type of wing that is shaped like a triangle. This plane has deltas, with a thick airfoil to keep it in flight!

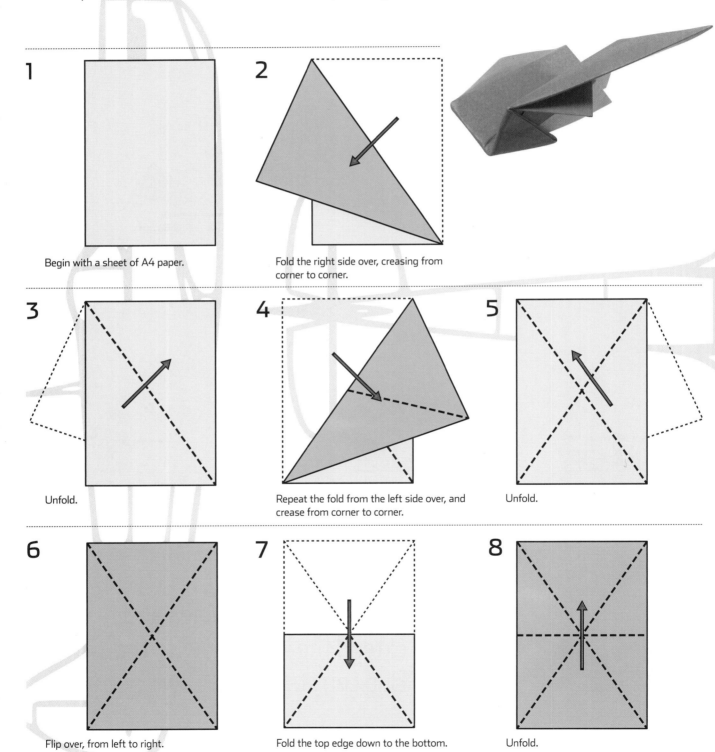

1
Begin with a sheet of A4 paper.

2
Fold the right side over, creasing from corner to corner.

3
Unfold.

4
Repeat the fold from the left side over, and crease from corner to corner.

5
Unfold.

6
Flip over, from left to right.

7
Fold the top edge down to the bottom.

8
Unfold.

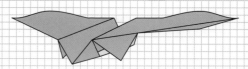

9

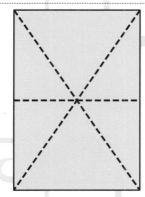

Flip over, from left to right.

10

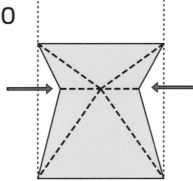

Tap the centre of the 'X' and then push in from the sides, folding in one side completely, then the other side as shown.

11

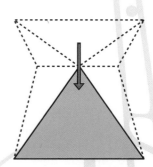

Press firmly down on the top to make a triangle.

12

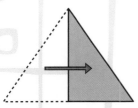

Fold the left side over to and even with the right side.

13

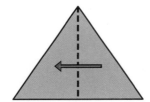

Unfold.

14

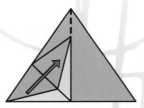

Fold the top layer on the left side up to the centre crease.

15

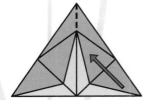

Fold the top layer on the right side up to the centre crease.

16

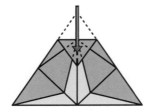

Fold the top point down so that the crease is even with the last two folds.

17

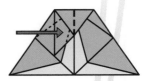

Fold the top layer on the left side over to the centre crease.

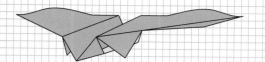

18

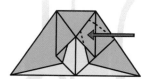

Fold the top layer on the right side over to the centre crease.

19

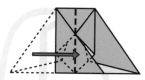

Fold the left side over to the right side as shown.

20

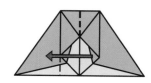

Unfold.

21

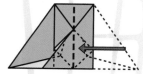

Fold the right side over to the left side as shown.

22

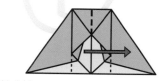

Unfold.

23

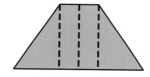

Flip over, from left to right.

24

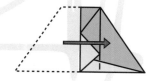

Fold the left side over to the right side.

Insert a finger into the delta wings and make them puffy. You may need to put a little up elevator on this plane. It's a nice slow flyer.

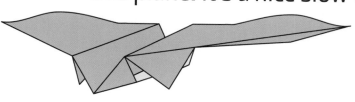

Alien Lander

If spacemen need a scout craft, so do any alien races we may encounter. This plane looks like it came straight out of a science-fiction comic book. But it's even better than that because it really flies!

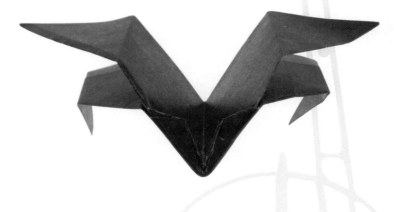

1

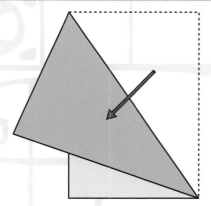

Begin with a sheet of A4 paper.

2

Fold the right side over, creasing from corner to corner.

3

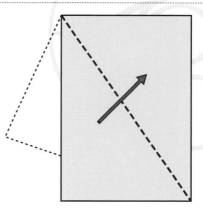

Unfold.

4

Fold the left side over, creasing from corner to corner.

5

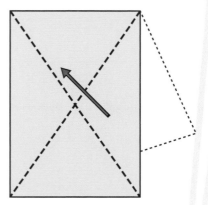

Unfold.

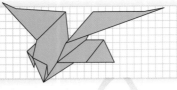

Alien Lander

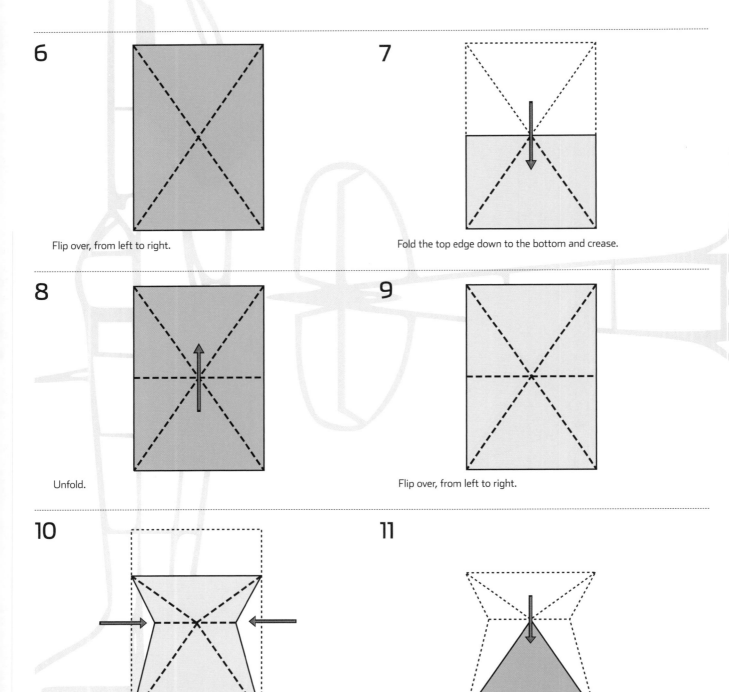

6

Flip over, from left to right.

7

Fold the top edge down to the bottom and crease.

8

Unfold.

9

Flip over, from left to right.

10

Tap the centre of the 'X' and then push in from the sides, folding in one side completely, then the other side as shown.

11

Press firmly down on the top to make a triangle.

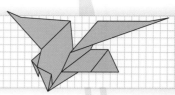

12

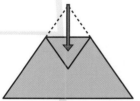

Fold the point down 5 cm (2 inches) and crease.

13

Fold the point back up.

14

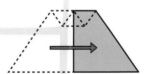

Fold the left side over to and even with the right side and crease.

15

Unfold.

16

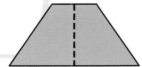

Flip over, from left to right.

17

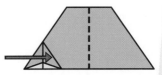

Fold the top layer on the left over to the right 3.5 cm (1.4 inches).

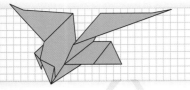

Alien Lander

18

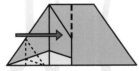

Fold the top left layer over to and even with the centre crease as shown.

19

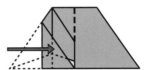

Fold the lower left layer over to and even with the centre crease as shown.

20

Fold the top layer on the right over to the left 3.5 cm (1.4 inches).

21

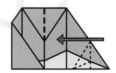

Fold the top right layer over to and even with the centre crease as shown.

22

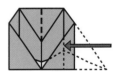

Fold the lower right layer over to the centre crease as shown.

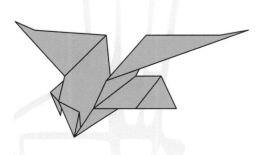

The Alien Lander may need a little twisting up of the ends in order to operate in our atmosphere. It will make a nice three-point landing on our planet!

Nakamura Lock

I only wish I had come up with this classic design myself. I am still trying to find out who did so originally, as it appears in many books about paper planes. The Nakamura Lock is a truly graceful flyer, and worth including in any book on paper planes!

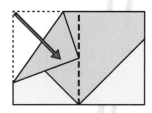

1

Begin with a sheet of A4 paper.

2

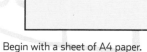

Fold the left side over to and even with the right side.

3

Unfold.

4

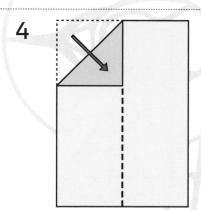

Fold the top left corner down to the centre crease as shown.

5

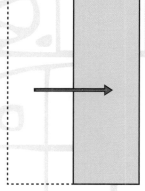

Fold the top right corner down to the centre crease as shown.

6

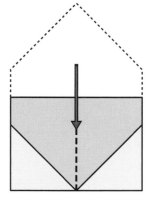

Fold the top point down to the bottom edge.

7

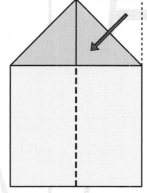

Fold the top left corner down to the centre of the vertical crease.

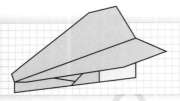
8

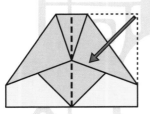

Fold the top right corner down to the centre of the vertical crease.

9

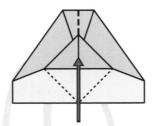

Fold the point up to lock in the sides as shown.

10

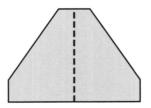

Flip over, from left to right.

11

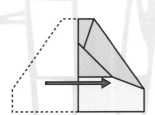

Fold the left side over to and even with the right side.

12

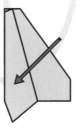

Fold the top right edge over to and even with the left edge as shown.

13

Flip over, from left to right.

14

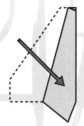

Fold the top left edge over to and even with the right edge as shown.

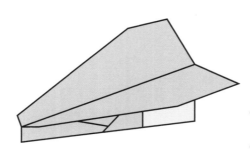

Pop the wings up, and grip the fuselage near the middle. Give the plane a good throw and watch it soar!

Mighty Mite

This little aeroplane is a great performer! Compact and strong, it can take a lot of punishment and still keep flying. Give it a try and you will see how the Mighty Mite earned its name!

1

Begin with a sheet of A4 paper.

2

Fold the left side over to and even with the right side.

3

Unfold.

4

Fold the top edge down to and even with the bottom edge.

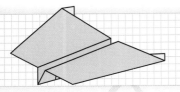

Mighty Mite

5

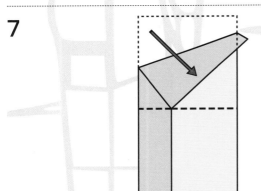

Unfold.

6

Fold the left side over to the centre vertical crease.

7

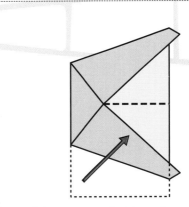

Fold the top left corner down to the intersection as shown.

8

Fold the bottom left corner up to the intersection as shown.

9

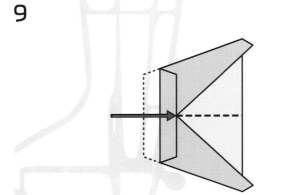

Flip fold the left side over to the intersection.

10

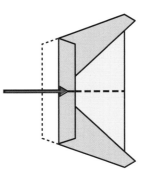

Flip fold the left side over again.

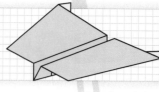

11

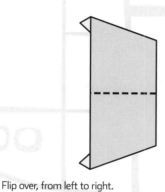

Flip over, from left to right.

12

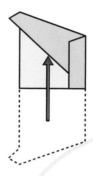

Fold the bottom edge up to and even with the top edge.

13

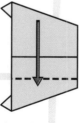

Fold the top layer down, leaving 3.5 cm (1.4 inches) for the fuselage.

14

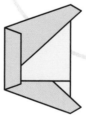

Flip over, from left to right.

15

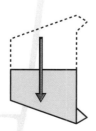

Fold the top edge down to and even with the bottom edge.

Put a small positive dihedral on the wings, and you have your Mighty Mite!

Scoop

As you can see, the Scoop has a lot in common with the Mighty Mite. Although the Scoop is not as tough, it is still a good flyer to have fun with!

1

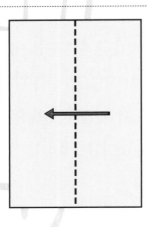

Begin with a sheet of A4 paper.

2

Fold the left side over to and even with the right side.

3

Unfold.

4

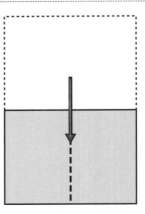

Fold the top edge down to and even with the bottom edge.

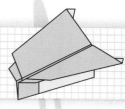

5

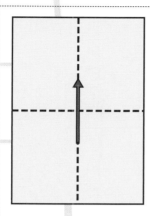

Unfold.

6

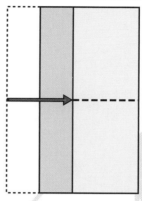

Fold the left side over to the centre vertical crease.

7

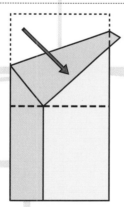

Fold the top left corner down to the intersection.

8

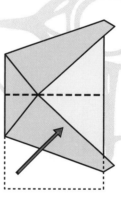

Fold the bottom left corner up to the intersection.

9

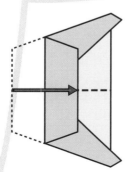

Fold the left side over to the right side, pivoting along the intersection.

10

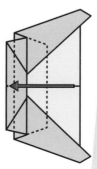

Take the right edge just created and fold it to the left 3.25 cm (1.25 inches) as shown.

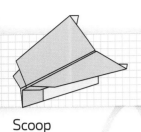

Scoop

11

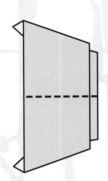

Flip over, from left to right.

12

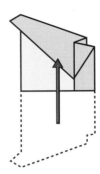

Fold the bottom edge up to and even with the top edge.

13

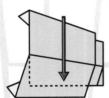

Fold the top layer down so that the right side of the fold is even with the bottom edge.

14

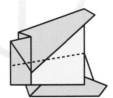

Flip over, from left to right.

15

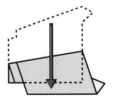

Fold the top edge down to and even with the bottom edge.

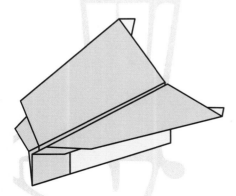

Elevate the Scoop's wings to a slight positive dihedral and it is ready for take-off!

Flying Fox

A flying fox is a large bat, and it has large ears, just like this plane. Make sure to puff out this Flying Fox's 'ears', as that will give it greater lift!

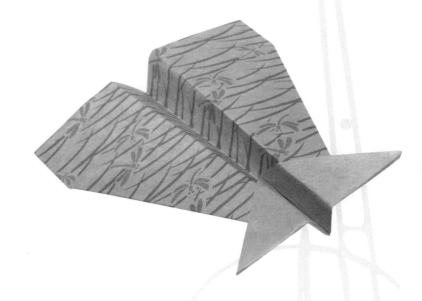

1

Begin with a sheet of A4 paper.

2

Fold the left side over to and even with the right side.

3

Unfold.

4

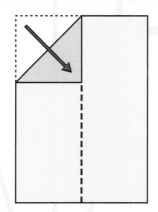

Fold the top left corner down to and even with the centre crease.

5

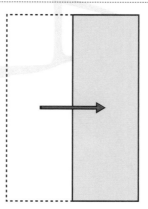

Fold the top right corner down to and even with the centre crease.

6

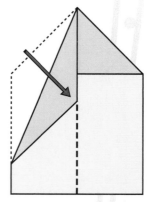

Fold the left angled side down to the centre crease.

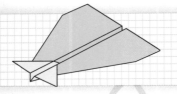

Flying Fox

7

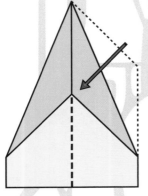

Fold the right angled side down to the centre crease.

8

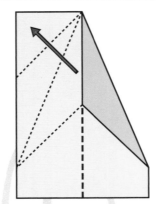

Unfold both folds on the left side.

9

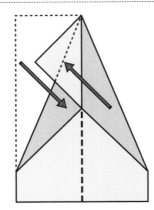

Fold in the crease closest to the centre, and fold back the other crease as shown.

10

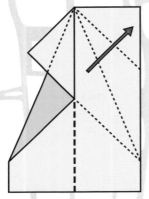

Unfold both folds on the right side.

11

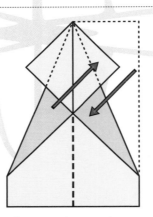

Fold in the crease closest to the centre, and fold back the other crease as shown.

12

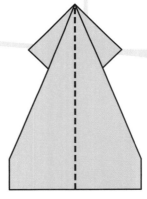

Flip over, from left to right.

13

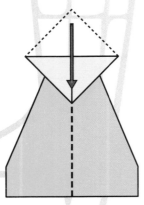

Fold the top point down, creating a line between the two corners as shown.

14

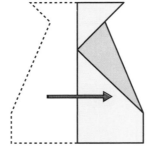

Fold the left side over to and even with the right side.

15

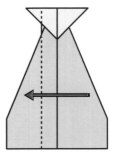

Fold the top layer on the right side over to the left side, leaving 2.5 cm (1 inch) for the fuselage.

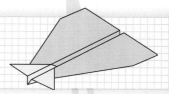

16

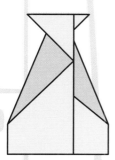

Flip over, from left to right.

17

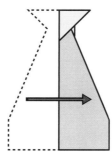

Fold the left side over to the right, leaving
2.5 cm (1 inch) for the fuselage.

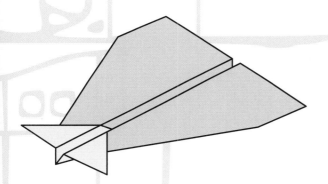

Straighten the wings, insert a
finger into each ear to puff them
up, and you're ready to soar!

Gullwing

This plane has wings shaped in the style of a gull. Gull wings have been the inspiration for many aeroplane designs throughout the years, and you can even see car doors that look like them too!

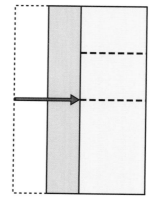

1

Begin with a sheet of A4 paper.

2

Fold the left side over to and even with the right side.

3

Unfold.

4

Fold the top edge down to and even with the bottom edge.

5

Unfold.

6

Fold the top edge down to the centre crease.

7

Unfold.

8

Fold the left side over to and even with the centre vertical crease.

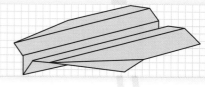

9

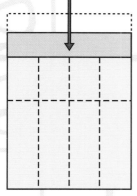

Unfold.

10

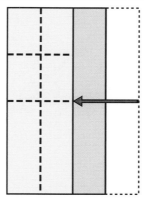

Fold the right side over to and even with the centre vertical crease.

11

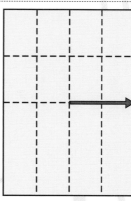

Unfold.

12

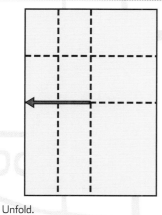

Fold the top edge down to and even with the first horizontal crease.

13

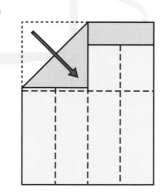

Fold the top left corner down to and even with the centre vertical crease.

14

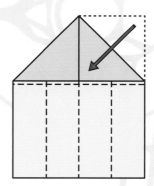

Fold the top right corner down to and even with the centre vertical crease.

15

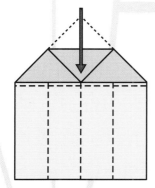

Fold the top point down to and even with the two previous folds.

16

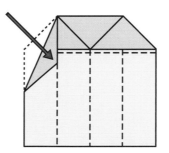

Fold the left angled side alongside the first vertical crease.

17

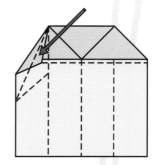

Squash fold the edge as shown.

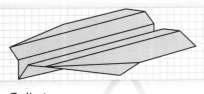

Gullwing

18

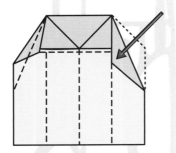

Fold the right angled side alongside the first vertical crease.

19

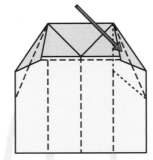

Squash fold the edge as shown.

20

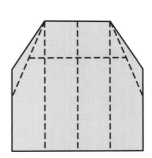

Flip over, from left to right.

21

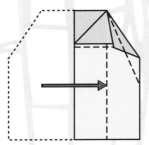

Fold the left side over to and even with the right side.

22

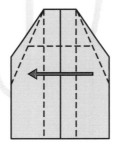

Fold the top layer over to the left, halfway across the top edge.

23

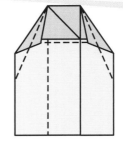

Flip over, from left to right.

24

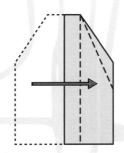

Fold the left side over to and even with the right side.

Pop open the wings as shown, and make sure they are angled alike. A very sensitive flyer, the Gullwing only requires a slow throw to send it cruising!

Vector

Named Vector for the capital 'V' it resembles, this plane has an otherworldly appearance. It is an unusual aircraft in that it has twin wings on each side.

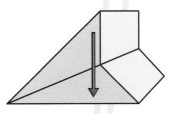

1

Begin with a sheet of A4 paper.

2

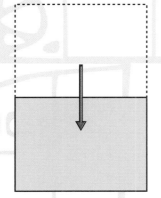

Fold the top edge down to the bottom edge.

3

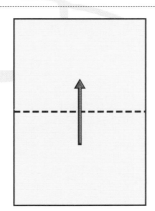

Unfold.

4

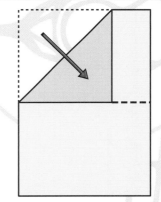

Fold the top left corner down to the centre crease.

5

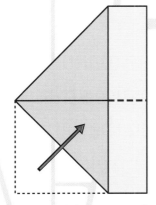

Fold the bottom left corner up to the centre crease.

6

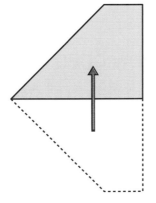

Fold the bottom edge up to and even with the top edge.

7

Fold the top layer down to and even with the bottom edge as shown.

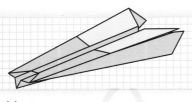

Vector

8

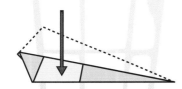

Continue by folding the top edge of this layer to the bottom edge as shown.

9

Flip over, from left to right.

10

Fold the top layer down to and even with the bottom edge as shown.

11

Continue by folding the top edge of this layer to the bottom edge as shown.

12

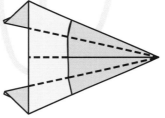

Open up, so that the view shown is the view from above.

13

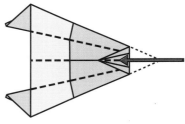

Fold the right point to the left 5 cm (2 inches).

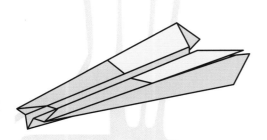

Now open up the wings, expand them a little, and give Vector a nice straight toss. If it dives, then open the wings up further, or give it a bit of up elevator.

Cat's Ears

This plane's forward rudders remind me of a cat's ears, so it was easy to come up with a name for it. Although the Cat's Ears is a little difficult to trim for flight, I am sure by now you are up to the task!

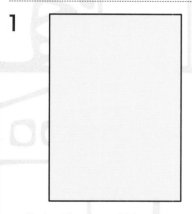

1

Begin with a sheet of A4 paper.

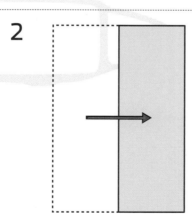

2

Fold the left side over to and even with the right side.

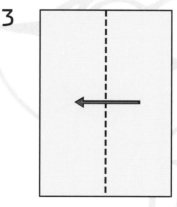

3

Unfold.

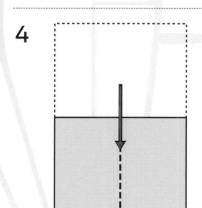

4

Fold the top edge down to and even with the bottom edge.

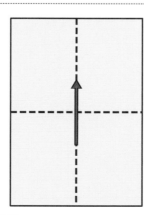

5

Unfold.

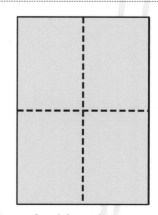

6

Flip over, from left to right.

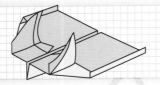
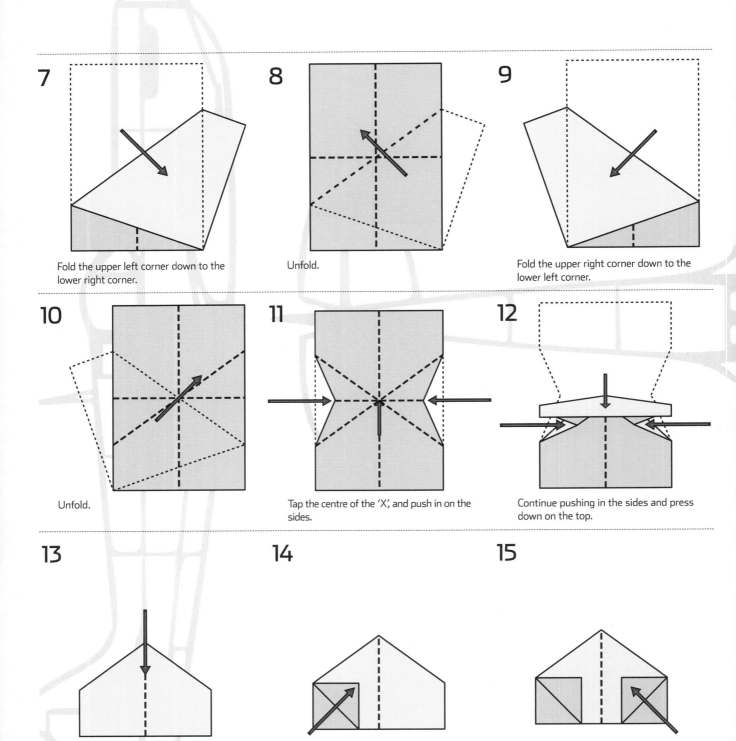

7

Fold the upper left corner down to the lower right corner.

8

Unfold.

9

Fold the upper right corner down to the lower left corner.

10

Unfold.

11

Tap the centre of the 'X', and push in on the sides.

12

Continue pushing in the sides and press down on the top.

13

Continue pressing down on the top until it looks like a little house.

14

Fold the upper layer of the lower left corner up until the top edge of the fold is horizontal.

15

Fold the upper layer of the lower right corner up until the top edge of the fold is horizontal.

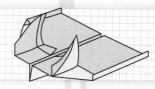

16

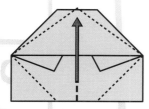

Fold the upper layer of the bottom edge up until it matches the horizontal edges just made.

17

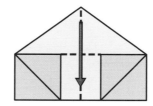

Unfold.

18

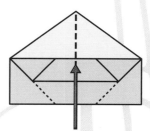

Fold the bottom edge up to the crease just created.

19

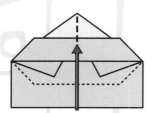

Flip fold up along the crease.

20

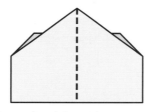

Flip over, from left to right.

21

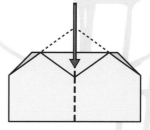

Fold the point down until it matches the level of the layer below.

22

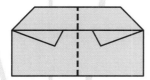

Flip over, from left to right.

23

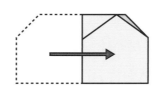

Fold the left side over to and even with the right side.

24

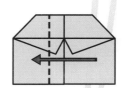

Fold the top layer on the right over to the left until the two triangles meet as shown.

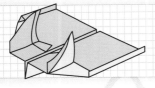

Cat's Ears

25

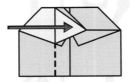

Take the top left layer over to the right as far as it can go, making sure the crease is vertical.

26

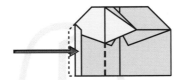

Fold the left edge over to the right 1 cm (0.4 inches).

27

Flip over, from left to right.

28

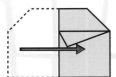

Fold the left side over to the right side until it matches the layer below on the left side.

29

Take the top right layer over to the left as far as it can go, making sure the crease is vertical.

30

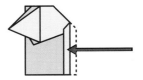

Fold the right edge over to the left 1 cm (0.4 inches).

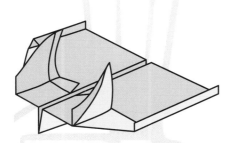

Straighten the wings, and curve the forward rudders by drawing a thumbnail along the inside of the 'cat's ears' to make them curve. Be sure to make them even and you will get a good flight!

Interceptor

S mall and swift, the Interceptor accelerates to a fine height with a strong throw. Be careful to make sure that the angles are sharp and even!

1

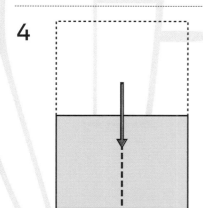

Begin with a sheet of A4 paper.

2

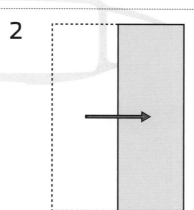

Fold the left side over to and even with the right side.

3

Unfold.

4

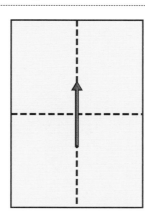

Fold the top edge down to and even with the bottom edge.

5

Unfold.

6

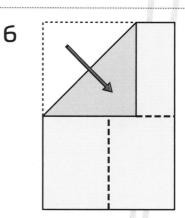

Fold the top left corner down to the centre horizontal crease.

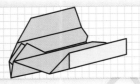

Interceptor

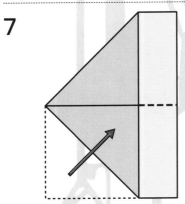

7

Fold the bottom left corner up to the centre horizontal crease.

8

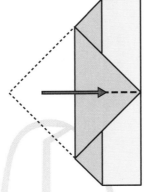

Fold the left point over to the right side.

9

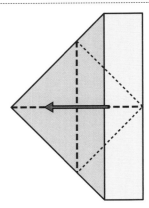

Unfold.

10

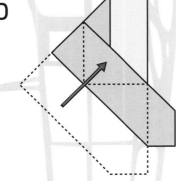

Fold the left point up to the crease located along the angled side and crease. Be sure to keep it even along the angled edge.

11

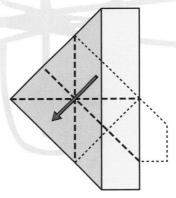

Unfold.

12

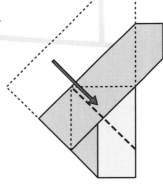

Fold the left point down to the crease located along the angled side. Be sure to keep it even along the angled edge.

13

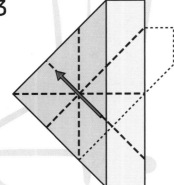

Unfold.

14

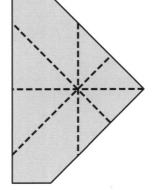

Flip over, from left to right.

15

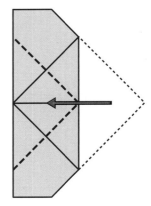

Fold the right point to the left side.

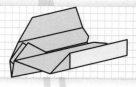

16

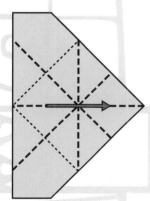

Unfold.

17

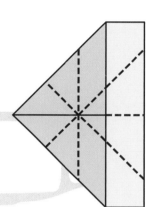

Flip over, from left to right.

18

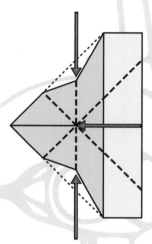

Press down in the centre, and push in on the sides as shown.

19

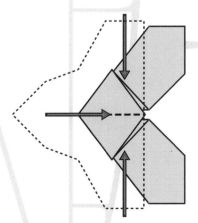

Continue pushing in on the sides, and press down on the top.

20

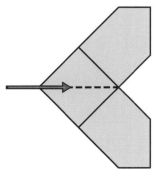

Continue pressing down on the top until the shape shown above appears.

21

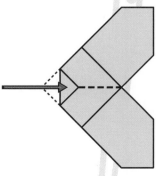

Fold the left point over to the right 2.5 cm (1 inch)

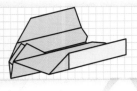

Interceptor

22

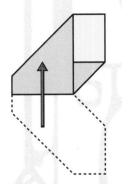

Fold the bottom edge up to and even with the top edge.

23

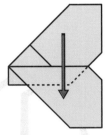

Fold the top layer down as far as possible on the left side, making sure the wing is horizontal.

24

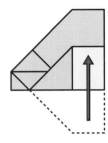

Fold the bottom edge up until it matches the bottom edge of the layer below.

25

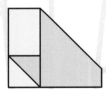

Flip over, from left to right.

26

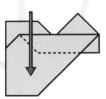

Fold the top down as far as possible on the right side, making sure the wing is horizontal.

27

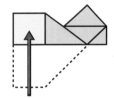

Fold the bottom edge up until it matches the bottom edge of the layer below.

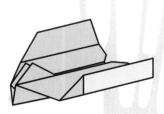

Pop up the wings and extend the winglets vertically. Take the Interceptor by the nose, give it a good strong throw, and watch it quickly gain altitude!

Moth

This model is called the Moth for two reasons. First, the 'feelers' in the front remind me of a moth. Second, when it's in the air, depending on how the feelers are positioned, the waggle of its wings makes the plane seem even more like an insect!

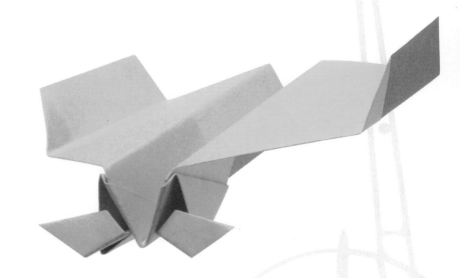

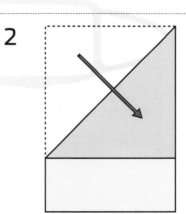

1

Begin with a sheet of A4 paper.

2

Fold the top left corner down to and even with the right side.

3

Unfold.

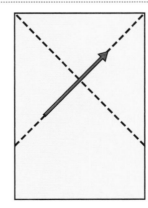

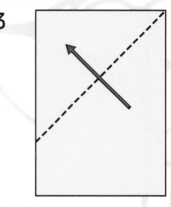

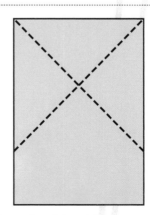

4

Now fold the right corner down to and even with the left side.

5

Unfold.

6

Flip over from left to right.

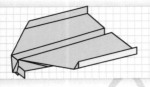

Moth

7

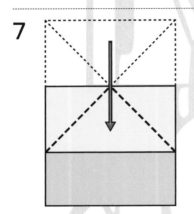

Fold the top down so that it is even with the creases.

8

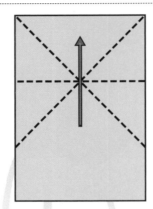

Unfold.

9

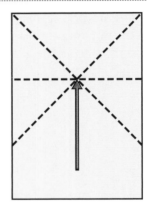

Flip it over and press at the centre of all the creases.

10

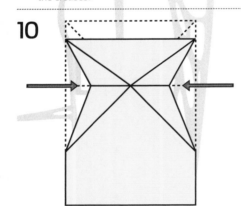

Press the sides in.

11

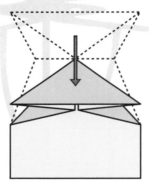

Push down on the top, folding in the sides as shown.

12

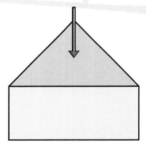

Keep pressing down on the top until it looks like a little house as shown.

13

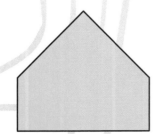

Flip over, from left to right.

14

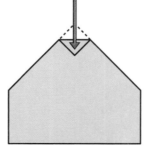

Fold the point down 2.5 cm (1 inch).

15

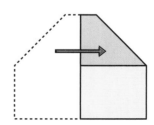

Fold the left side over to and even with the right side.

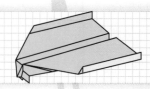

Moth

16

Lift the top layer up and even with the left side and crease.

17

Unfold.

18

Fold the lower edge of the top layer up to the crease just made.

19

Flip fold along the same crease.

20

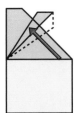

Flip fold again.

21

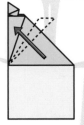

Fold all the layers up along the left side as shown.

22

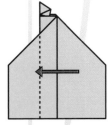

Fold the top right layer over to the left, pivoting along the upper right corner.

23

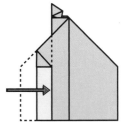

Fold the left edge over to the right, making it even with the fuselage below.

24

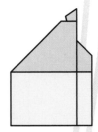

Flip over, from left to right.

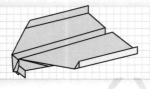

Moth

25

Lift the top layer up and even with the right side and crease.

26

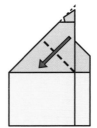

Unfold.

27

Fold the lower edge of the top layer up to the crease just made.

28

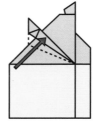

Flip fold along that same crease.

29

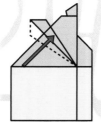

Flip fold again.

30

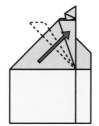

Fold all the layers up along the right side as shown.

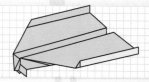

31

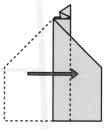

Fold the top left layer over to the right, pivoting along the upper left corner.

32

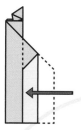

Fold the right edge over to the left, making it even with the fuselage below.

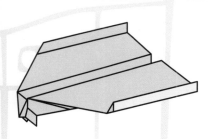

There are quite a few steps to the Moth, but the result is an interesting flyer! Pop up the wings, make sure the winglets are straight up, and have fun with the 'feelers' in the Moth's mouth. Depending on how you position them, the 'feelers' will alter the flight. Feel free to adjust them at will and experiment!

Space Cruiser

A little unearthly in its design, Space Cruiser was meant for interstellar travel! Sleek and speedy, this is a great flyer!

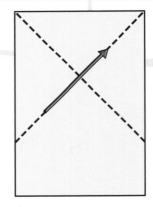

1

Begin with a sheet of A4 paper.

2

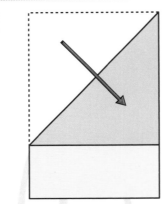

Fold the top left corner down to and even with the right side.

3

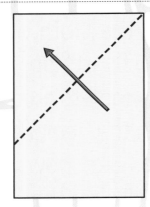

Unfold.

4

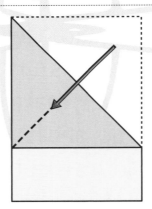

Now fold the right corner down to and even with the left side.

5

Unfold.

6

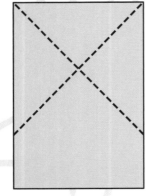

Flip over, from left to right.

7

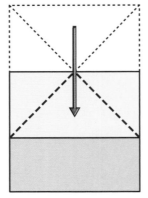

Fold the top down so that it is even with the creases.

8

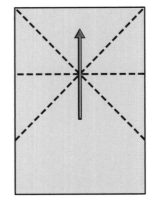

Unfold.

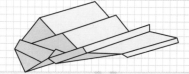

9

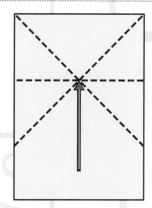

Flip over and press at the centre of all the creases.

10

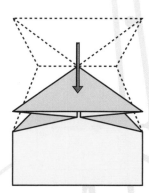

Press the sides in.

11

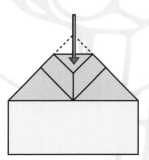

Push down on the top, folding in the sides.

12

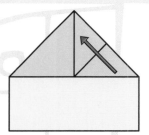

Fold the top right section up to the centre point as shown.

13

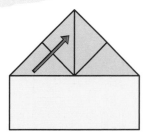

Fold the top left section up to the centre point.

14

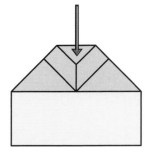

Fold the top down 4 cm (1.6 inches).

15

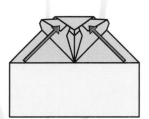

Insert the two sections into the two pockets as shown.

16

Press down on the top to make sure the sections are in firmly.

17

Fold the left side over to and even with the right side.

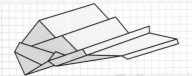

Space Cruiser

18

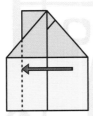

Fold the top layer on the right over to the left as far as possible on the top edge, keeping it even on the bottom edge.

19

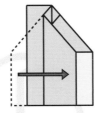

Fold the left side over to the right, watching the top angle, thus completing the diamond shape as shown at the top point of the diagram.

20

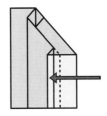

Fold that layer back 1 cm (0.4 inches).

21

Flip over, from left to right.

22

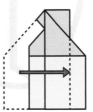

Fold the top layer on the left over to the right as far as possible on the top edge, keeping it even on the bottom edge.

23

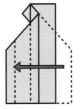

Fold the right side over to the left, watching the top angle, thus completing the diamond shape as shown at the top point of the diagram.

24

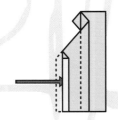

Fold that layer back 1 cm (0.4 inches).

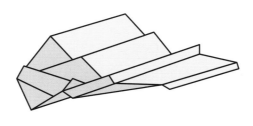

Unfold, extending the wings so that the plane is fairly flat. Grab the Space Cruiser by the nose and let it fly!

UFO

This is an old design, and is known by various names. You will recognise some of the early steps from the Space Cruiser, but this plane flies totally differently, and its method of launching is original too. I have always called it the UFO, because it looks so unusual to me!

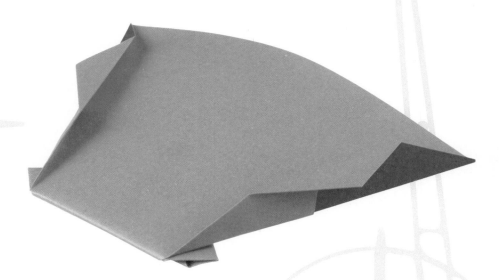

1

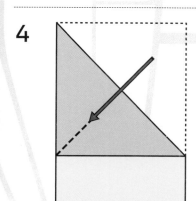

Begin with a sheet of A4 paper.

2

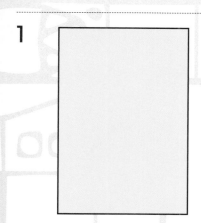

Fold the top left corner down to and even with the right side.

3

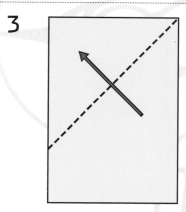

Unfold.

4

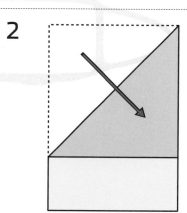

Fold the right corner down to and even with the left side.

5

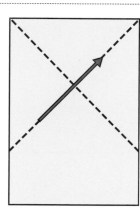

Unfold.

6

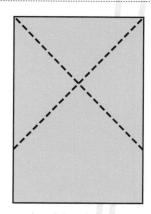

Flip over, from left to the right.

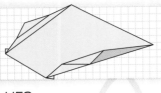

UFO

7
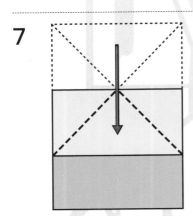
Fold the top down so that it is even with the creases.

8
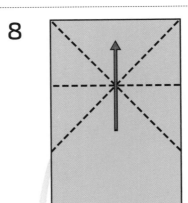
Unfold.

9
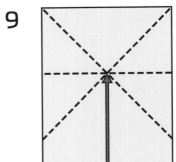
Flip over and press at the centre of all the creases.

10
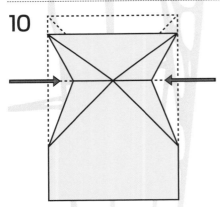
Press the sides in.

11
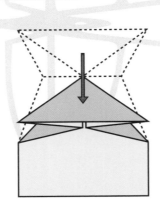
Push down on the top, folding in the sides.

12
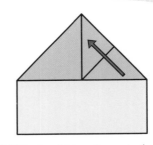
Fold the top right section up to the centre point as shown.

13
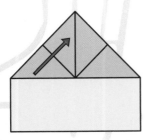
Fold the top left section up to the centre point as shown.

14
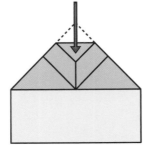
Fold the top down 4 cm (1.6 inches).

15
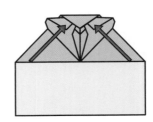
Insert the two sections into the two pockets as shown.

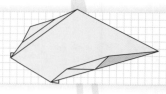

16

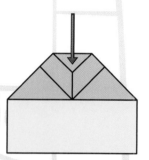

Press down on the top to make sure the sections are in firmly.

17

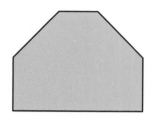

Flip over, from left to right.

18

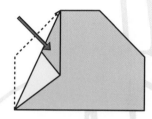

Fold the left side over, creasing from the top left corner to the bottom left corner.

19

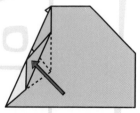

Fold back to the left as shown.

20

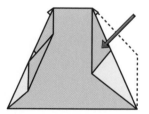

Fold the right side in, creasing from the top right corner down to the bottom right corner.

21

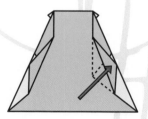

Fold back to the right as shown.

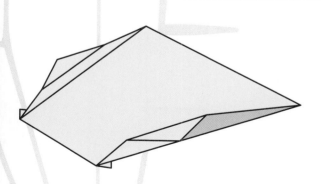

The UFO is an interesting flyer with a nice, smooth glide. To launch, put your fingers into the pocket underneath the wing, then flip your hand forward, letting the plane slide off your hand.

Barrel Roll

A barrel roll is an aviation manoeuvre where an aeroplane rotates around its axis. This plane, the Barrel Roll, not only looks like a barrel split in half, but it does a half barrel roll almost every time you fly it!

1

Begin with a sheet of A4 paper.

2

Fold the left side over to and even with the right side.

3

Unfold.

4

Fold the left side over to the centre crease.

5

Unfold.

6

Fold the left side over to the crease just created.

7

Unfold.

8

Fold the left side over to the crease just created.

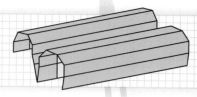

Barrel Roll

9

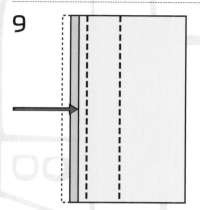

Flip fold the paper over along the left side, keeping the same width.

10

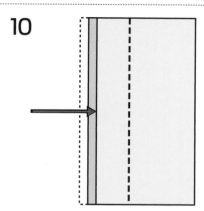

Flip fold the paper over along the left side, keeping the same width.

11

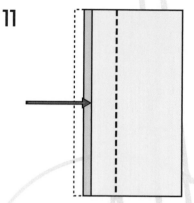

Flip fold the paper over along the left side, keeping the same width.

12

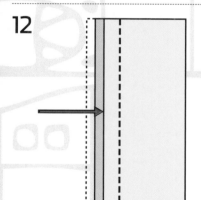

Flip fold the paper over along the left side, keeping the same width.

13

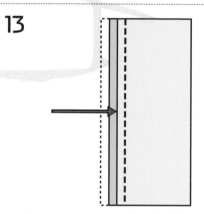

Flip fold the paper over along the left side, keeping the same width.

14

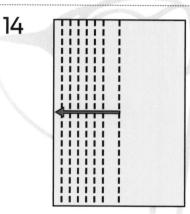

Unfold all.

15

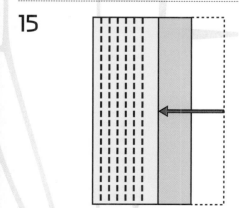

Fold the right side over to and even with the centre crease.

16

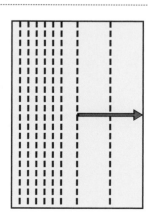

Unfold.

17

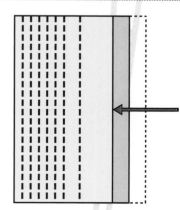

Fold the right side over to the crease just created.

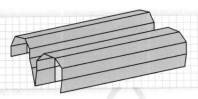

Barrel Roll

18 Unfold.

19 Fold the right side over to the crease just created.

20 Flip fold the paper over along the right side, keeping the same width.

21 Flip fold the paper over along the right side, keeping the same width.

22 Flip fold the paper over along the right side, keeping the same width.

23 Flip fold the paper over along the right side, keeping the same width.

24 Flip fold the paper over along the right side, keeping the same width.

25 Unfold all.

26 Fold the top edge down to and even with the bottom edge.

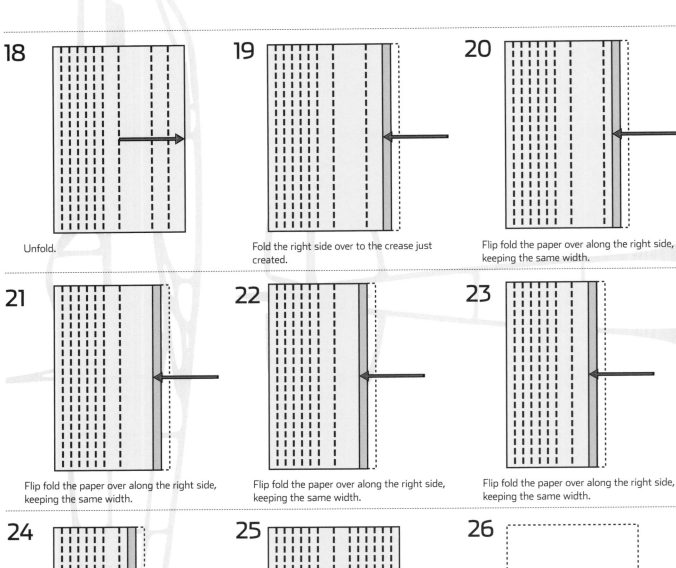
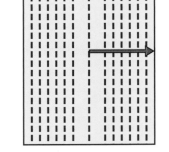
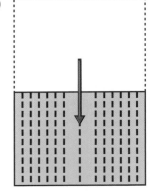

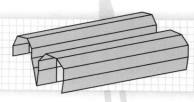

27

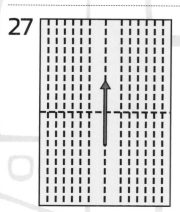

Unfold.

28

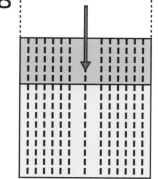

Fold the top edge down to the horizontal crease.

29

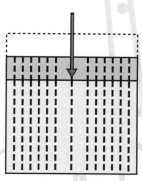

Fold the top edge down to the horizontal crease.

30

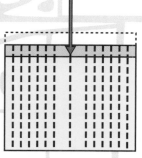

Fold the top edge down to the horizontal crease.

31

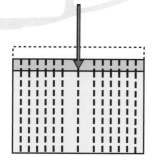

Flip fold the top edge down, keeping the same width.

32

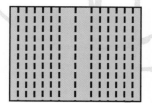

Flip over, from left to right.

33

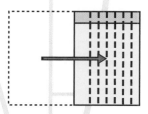

Fold the left side over to the right side.

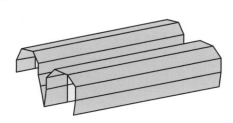

To make this plane live up to its name, form both wings to look like half barrels. Throw the heavy end first, and a half barrel roll will be promptly executed.

Flapper II

The Flapper II doesn't fly fast or far, but it does a nifty trick that gives it its name! This plane looks simple, but when it flies it's a lot of fun.

1

Begin with a sheet of A4 paper.

2

Fold the left side over to and even with the right side.

3

Unfold.

4

Rotate the paper 90 degrees, so that the long sides are on the top and bottom.

5

Fold the left side over to and even with the right side.

6

Unfold.

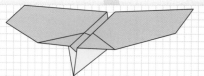

7

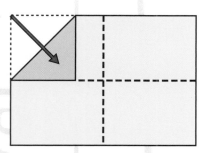

Fold the top left corner down to and even with the horizontal crease.

8

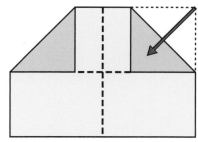

Fold the top right corner down to and even with the horizontal crease.

9

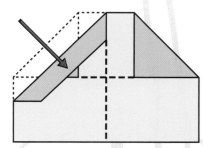

Take the left side and fold it as shown, keeping the upper right side even with the vertical crease.

10

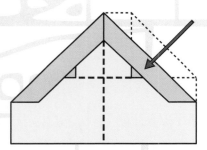

Take the right side and fold it as shown, keeping the upper left side even with the vertical crease.

11

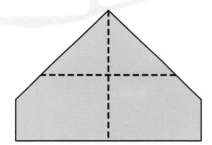

Flip over, from right to left.

12

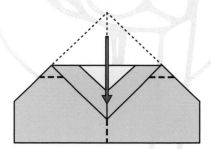

Fold the upper point down 8.5 cm (3.3 inches).

13

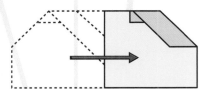

Fold the left side over to the right side.

14

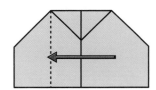

Using the top edge as a guide, fold the top layer back to the left side, exactly half the length of the top edge.

15

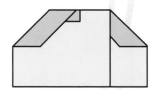

Flip over, from right to left.

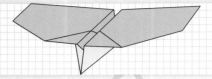

Flapper II

16

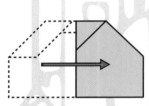

Again, using the top edge as a guide, fold the top layer back to the right side, exactly half the length of the top edge.

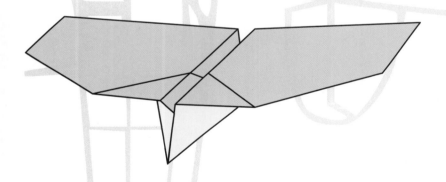

The Flapper II is now complete! Toss it gently, with a slight downward tilt, and it will flap its wings!

RTM

RTM (Return To Me) is such a cool-looking plane. Be careful when you fly it, though!

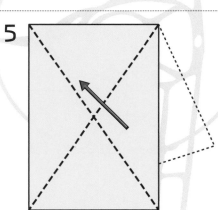

1

Begin with a sheet of A4 paper.

2

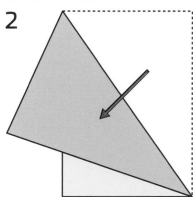

Fold the right side over, making a crease from the top left corner to the bottom right corner.

3

Unfold.

4

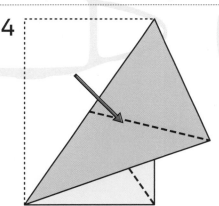

Fold the left side over, making a crease from the top right corner to the bottom left corner.

5

Unfold.

6

Flip over, from left to right.

7

Fold the left side over to the right side.

8

Unfold.

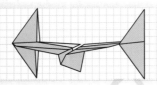

9

Flip over, from left to right.

10

Rotate the paper 90 degrees, so that the long sides are at the top and the bottom.

11

Press in at the centre.

12

Fold the sides in and the top down.

13

Press firmly down on the top to get the result shown.

14

Fold the left side over to and even with the right side.

15

Unfold.

16

Fold the top point down to and even with the bottom as shown.

17

Fold the top layer on the left over 4 cm (1.6 inches), following the angle of the paper as shown.

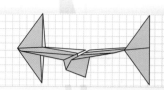

18

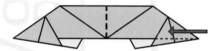

Repeat on the top layer on the right side.

19

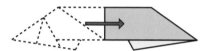

Fold in half again.

20

Fold the top layer on the right over 4 cm (1.6 inches), matching the layer below.

21

Fold the top wing over to the left, matching the angle shown.

22

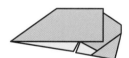

Flip over, from left to right.

23

Fold the left side over 4 cm (1.6 inches), matching the layer below.

24

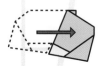

Fold the left wing over, matching the wings below.

The RTM is a trick flyer. Unfold the wings so they are level, and unfold the winglets so they are straight up and straight down. Tossed at a gentle angle into the sky, it will stall, flip over, and return to you!

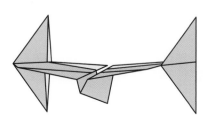

Step Pyramid

Everyone knows about the great pyramids of Egypt. But before the ancient Egyptians produced the giant smooth-sided triangle-shaped ones, they made pyramids that looked like a series of steps. This paper aeroplane replicates that building process, making a series of wings, one right behind the other.

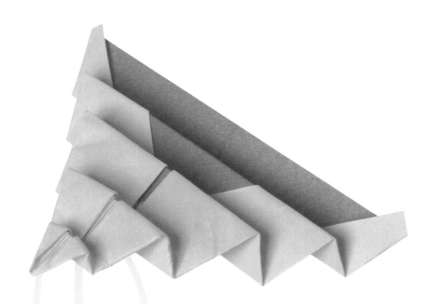

1

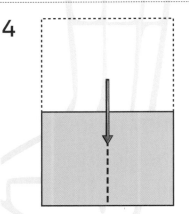

Begin with a sheet of A4 paper.

2

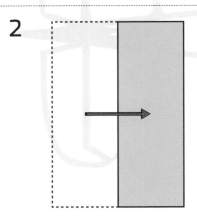

Fold the left side over to and even with the right side.

3

Unfold.

4

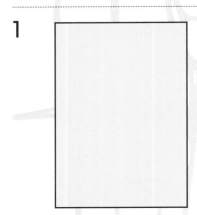

Fold the top edge down to and even with the bottom edge.

5

Unfold.

6

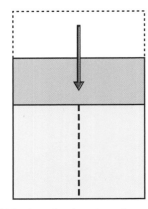

Fold the top edge down to and even with the centre horizontal crease.

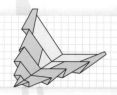

7

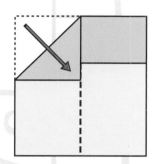

Fold the top left corner down to the vertical crease as shown.

8

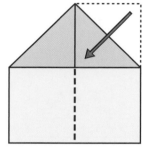

Fold the top right corner down to the vertical crease as shown.

9

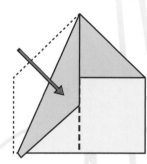

Fold the left angled side down to the vertical crease as shown.

10

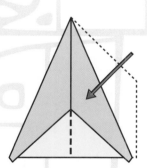

Fold the right angled side down to the vertical crease as shown.

11

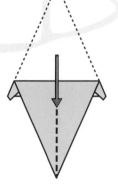

Fold the point down until only 3 cm (1.2 inches) remains in the first step.

12

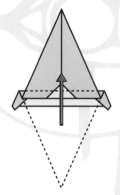

Fold the point back up, leaving 1.5 cm (0.6 inches) behind in that layer.

13

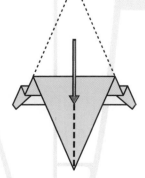

Fold the point down again, leaving 3 cm (1.2 inches) in this step.

14

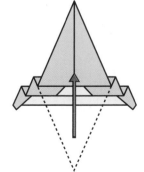

Fold up again, leaving another 1.5 cm (0.6 inches) behind in this layer.

15

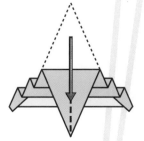

Fold the point down again, leaving another 3 cm (1.2 inches).

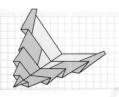

16

Fold the point back up, leaving another
1.5 cm (0.6 inches) behind.

17

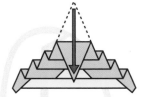

Fold the point down once more, again
leaving a 3 cm (1.2 inch) step.

18

Fold the point up once more, leaving
1.5 cm (0.6 inches) behind.

19

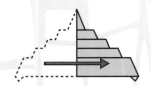

Fold the left side over to and even with
the right.

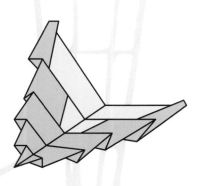

And there you go! You have completed
the Step Pyramid. To launch, keeping
a slight positive dihedral, lay your
forefinger down the centre crease.
Put your thumb underneath one wing,
and your middle finger under the other.
Raise your arm and, with a slight
snapping motion, release the plane
point first, level and straight ahead.
It will take some practice, but once you
master the moves, this is an accurate
and interesting flyer!

Annular Wing

Annular wings are an aviation oddity. Although they are full of promise and potential, no one has been really able to make them work on an actual aeroplane. But in the paper aeroplane world, they are easy to make and a lot of fun to fly!

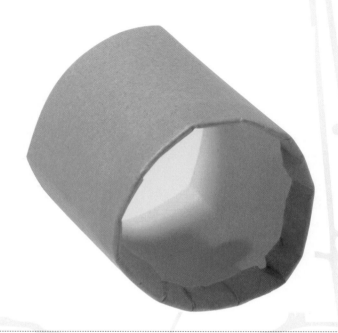

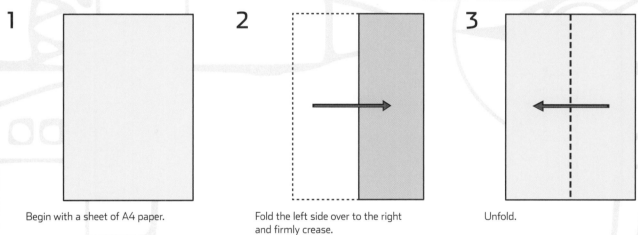

1
Begin with a sheet of A4 paper.

2
Fold the left side over to the right and firmly crease.

3
Unfold.

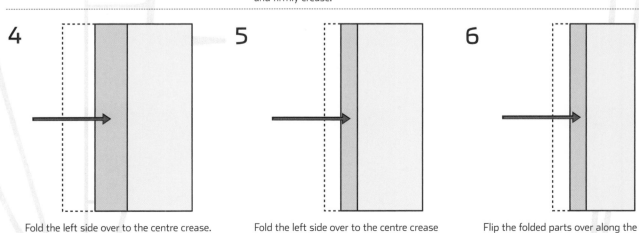

4
Fold the left side over to the centre crease.

5
Fold the left side over to the centre crease again.

6
Flip the folded parts over along the centre crease.

Annular Wing

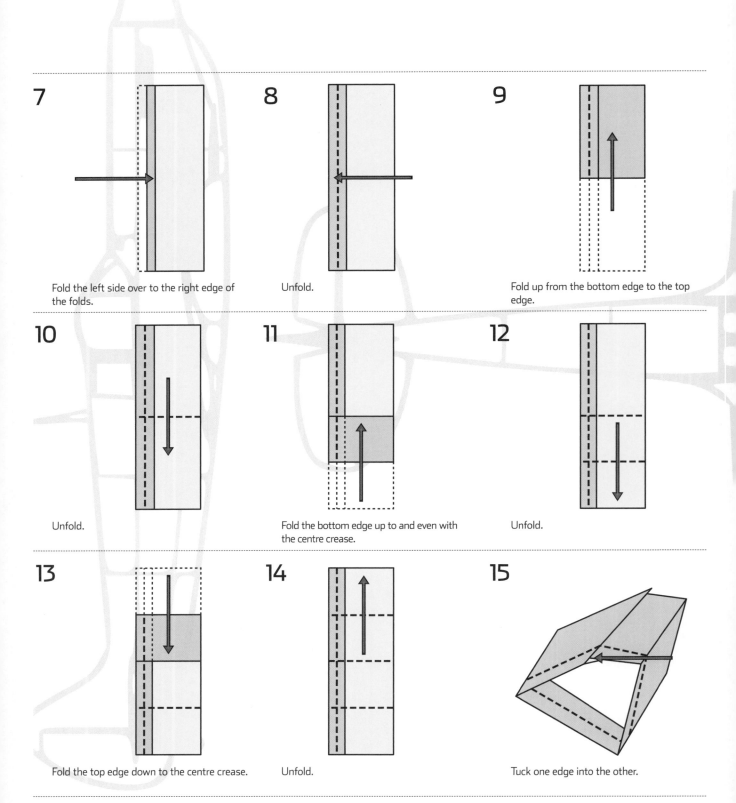

7

Fold the left side over to the right edge of the folds.

8

Unfold.

9

Fold up from the bottom edge to the top edge.

10

Unfold.

11

Fold the bottom edge up to and even with the centre crease.

12

Unfold.

13

Fold the top edge down to the centre crease.

14

Unfold.

15

Tuck one edge into the other.

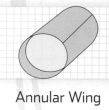

16

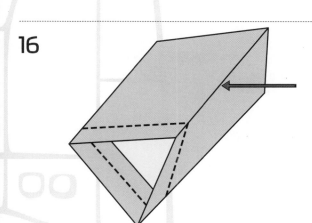

Push the edge into the other until a triangle is created.

17

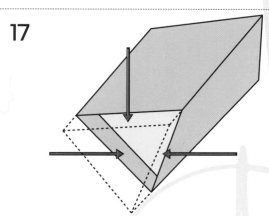

Tuck the end in, following the previous folds.

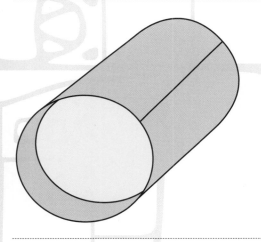

Round out the edge. Throw the heavy end first to fly the Annular Wing in a spiral motion like a football.

Apollo's Chariot

Apollo's Chariot is a closed wing version of the annular wing concept. The way it flies calls to mind Apollo's Golden Chariot as it raced across the sky.

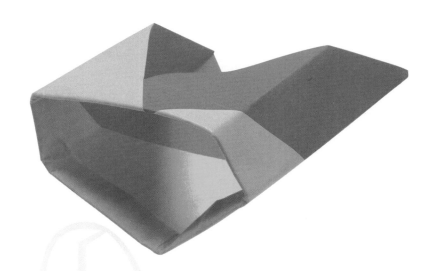

1

Begin with a sheet of A4 paper.

2

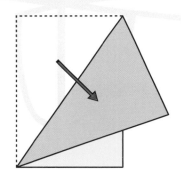

Fold the left side over, making a crease from corner to corner.

3

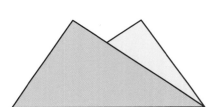

Rotate the paper until the long side is at the bottom as shown.

4

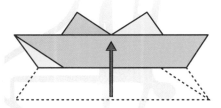

Fold the bottom edge up to the intersection as shown.

5

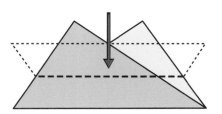

Unfold.

6

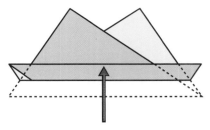

Fold the bottom edge up to the crease just created.

7

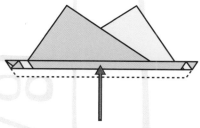

Fold the bottom edge up to the crease again.

8

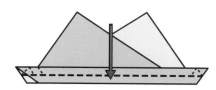

Unfold.

9

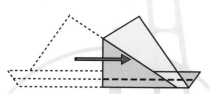

Fold the left side over to and even with the right side.

10

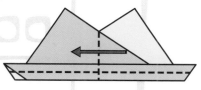

Unfold.

11

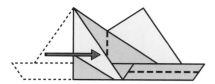

Fold the left side over, keeping it even with the bottom, and creating a crease to the top of the left point.

12

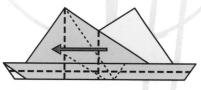

Unfold.

13

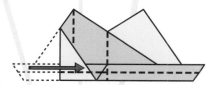

Fold the left side over until it meets the centre crease.

14

Unfold.

15

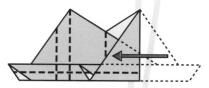

Fold the right side over, keeping it even with the bottom, and creating a crease to the top of the right point.

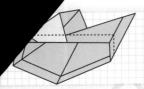

Apollo's Chariot

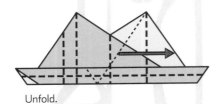

Unfold.

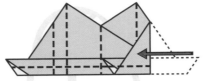

17

Fold the right side over to the centre crease.

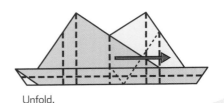

Unfold.

19

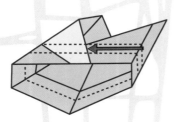

Curve the paper around, creating a pentagon shape, and tuck in the left and right ends.

20

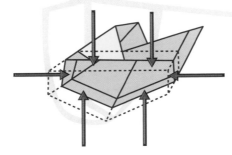

Tuck the edges inside to lock the plane together.

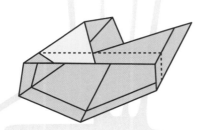

Launching Apollo's Chariot is a little different from other planes. You place it on your fingers, and fling it forward. It should shoot straight off!

El Diablo

El Diablo, another name for the devil, is an apt description for this little plane. It's tricky to master the folds and trim it for flight, so the name is well earned! Give it a try and have patience – you will be rewarded with a neat aeroplane!

1

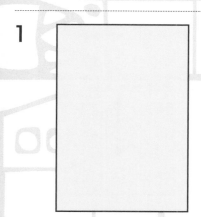

Begin with a sheet of A4 paper.

2

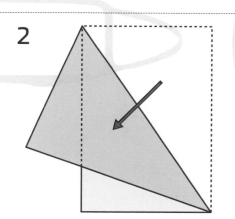

Fold the right side over, making a crease from the top left corner to the bottom right corner.

3

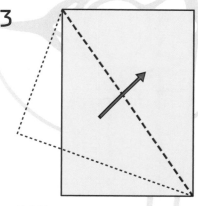

Unfold.

4

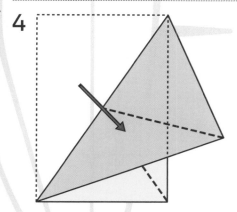

Fold the left side over, making a crease from the top right corner to the bottom left corner.

5

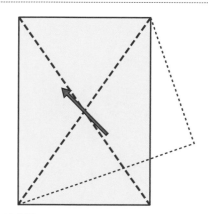

Unfold.

6

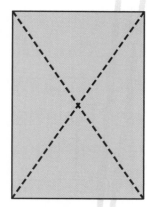

Flip over, from left to right.

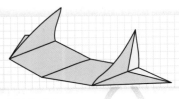

El Diablo

7

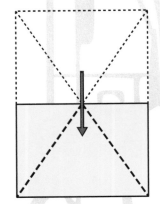

Fold the top edge down to and even with the bottom edge.

8

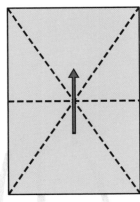

Unfold.

9

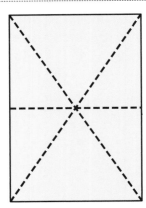

Flip over, from left to right.

10

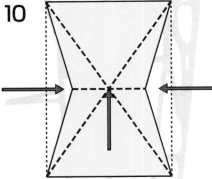

Press in at the point where all three lines intersect, and both left and right sides should pop up. Continue pressing them in.

11

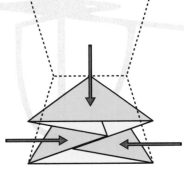

Continue pressing in the sides, one on top of the other, and pressing the top down on top of them as shown.

12

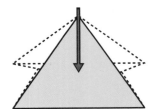

Continue until a pyramid is created.

13

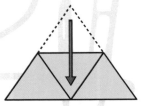

Fold the top point down to the bottom edge.

14

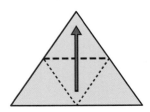

Unfold.

15

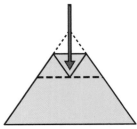

Fold the top point down to the crease just created.

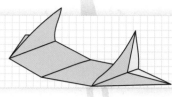

16

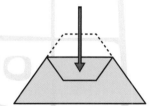

Flip fold along the crease.

17

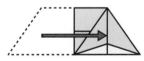

Fold the top left layer to the right as shown.

18

Fold the top right layer to the left as shown.

19

Flip over, from left to right.

20

Fold the left side over to and even with the right side.

21

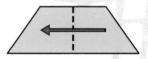

Unfold.

22

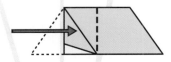

Fold the left side over to the centre crease.

23

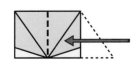

Fold the right side over to the centre crease.

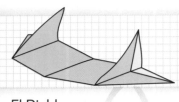

El Diablo

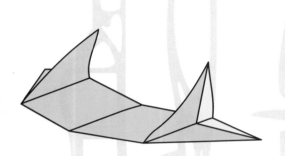

Now comes the tricky part. The lower wing tips should have a slight negative dihedral. The upper wing tips need to have a slight curve; you can accomplish this by dragging your thumbnail along the inner side of the tips. This will help stabilise the craft, and at the same time gives El Diablo its devilish horns.

El Diablo is another finger flicker to launch. Place your forefinger along the central crease and flick your hand straight ahead to send it airborne!

Bat

The Bat is another unusual flyer. It is so named because the wings look like a bat's wings. Launched with a gentle toss upwards, this craft prefers to fly upside down, quickly twisting into position.

1

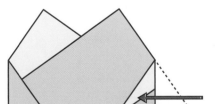

Begin with a sheet of A4 paper.

2

Fold the right side over, making a crease from the top left corner to the bottom right corner.

3

Rotate until the crease becomes the bottom edge.

4

Fold the left bottom corner in 6.5 cm (2.5 inches), keeping even along the bottom edge.

5

Fold the right bottom corner in 6.5 cm (2.5 inches), keeping even along the bottom edge.

6

Flip fold the bottom left corner up along the slanted edge as shown.

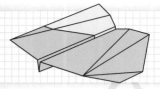

Bat

7

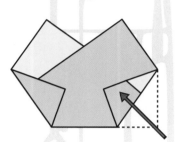

Flip fold the bottom right corner up along the slanted edge as shown.

8

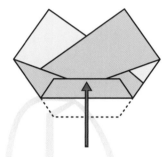

Fold the bottom edge up to meet the two inner corners of the triangles just created.

9

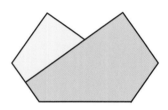

Flip over from left to right.

10

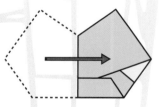

Fold the left side over to and even with the right side.

11

Fold the top layer from right to left, making a crease from the lower right corner to the top point as shown.

12

Unfold.

13

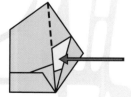

Fold the bottom angled edge from right to left to the crease just created.

14

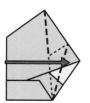

Unfold.

15

Take the first crease over to the top left corner, pivoting on the bottom right corner.

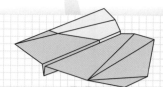

16

Unfold.

17

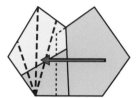

Fold the top layer from right to left, leaving 2 cm (0.75 inches) at the bottom edge, and 1.5 cm (0.6 inches) at the top for the fuselage.

18

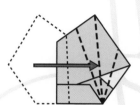

Unfold.

19

Flip over, from left to right.

20

Fold the top layer from left to right, making a crease from the lower left corner to the top point as shown.

21

Unfold.

22

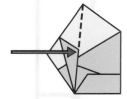

Fold the bottom angled edge from left to right to the crease just created.

23

Unfold.

24

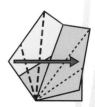

Take the first crease over to the top right corner, pivoting on the bottom left corner.

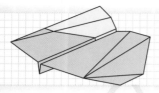

Bat

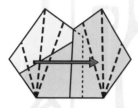

Fold the top layer from left to right, leaving
2 cm (0.75 inches) at the bottom edge and
1.5 cm (0.6 inches) at the top for the fuselage.

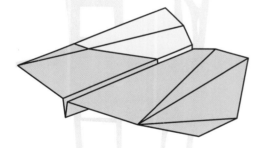

Using all the folds, angle the wings to
curve downwards, like a bat's wings.
Give the plane a gentle toss upwards,
and watch it go!

Vulture

Vultures are very efficient flyers. Their large wings allow them to soar effortlessly through the sky. While this plane does not have huge wings, it does incorporate a birdlike airfoil to increase lift.

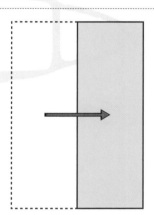

1

Begin with a sheet of A4 paper.

2

Fold the left side over to and even with the right side.

3

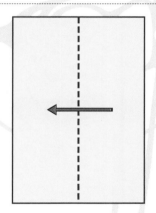

Unfold.

4

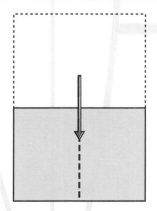

Fold the top edge down to and even with the bottom edge.

5

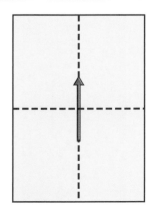

Unfold.

6

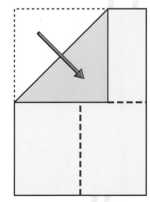

Fold the top left corner down to the centre horizontal crease.

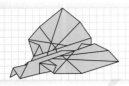

Vulture

7

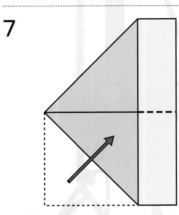

Fold the bottom left corner up to the centre horizontal crease.

8

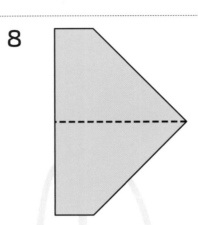

Flip over, from left to right.

9

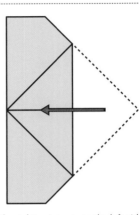

Fold the right point over to the left side.

10

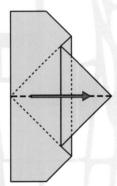

Fold the left point back to the right, within 1.5 cm (0.6 inches).

11

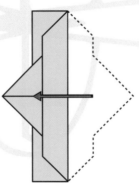

Fold the right point to the left, using the upper right and lower right corners as a guide, and crease.

12

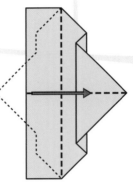

Unfold.

13

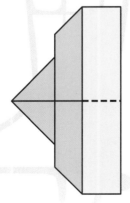

Flip over, from left to right.

14

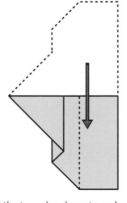

Fold the top edge down to and even with the bottom edge.

15

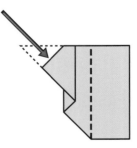

Inside reverse fold the upper left corner as shown.

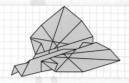
16

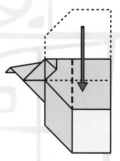

Inside reverse fold the previous fold as shown.

17

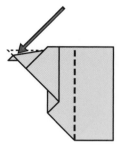

Reverse fold as shown.

18

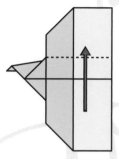

Fold the top layer from the bottom edge up, using the left point as a pivot as shown.

19

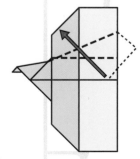

Fold the top edge down, matching the top edge of the layer below.

20

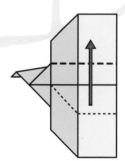

Unfold.

21

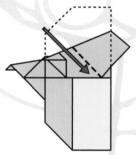

Fold the upper left angled edge to the layer edge.

22

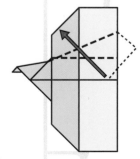

Unfold.

23

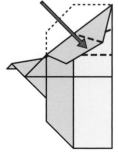

Fold the top layer down, making a crease between the upper right corner and the tip of the triangle, and crease.

24

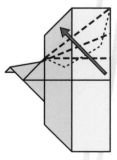

Unfold.

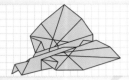

Vulture

25

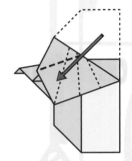

Fold the top layer down, making a crease between the lower right corner and the left angled corner.

26

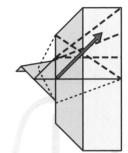

Unfold.

27

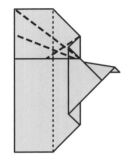

Flip over, from left to right.

28

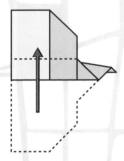

Fold the top layer from the bottom edge up, using the right point as a pivot as shown.

29

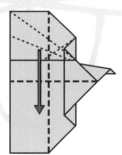

Unfold.

30

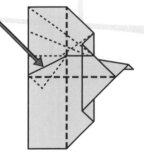

Inside reverse fold the tail as shown.

31

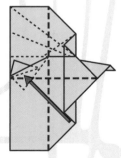

Another inside reverse fold pops the tail back up.

32

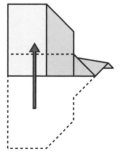

Fold the bottom edge up, matching the bottom edge of the layer below.

33

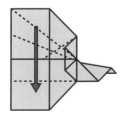

Fold the top edge down, matching the top edge of the layer below as shown.

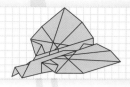

34

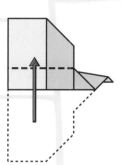

Unfold.

35

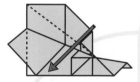

Fold the upper left angled edge to the layer edge as shown.

36

Unfold.

37

Fold the top layer down, making a crease between the upper left corner and the tip of the triangle as shown.

38

Unfold.

39

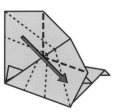

Fold the top layer down, making a crease between the lower left corner and the right angled corner as shown.

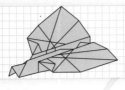

Vulture

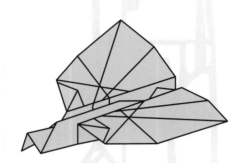

After all those folds, when you open up the wings, you should see that the combination of valley and mountain folds has produced a concave wing. The Vulture is hard to trim, but once you do, it will glide effortlessly with a gentle toss.